LJB

TRINITY BLOOD™

RAGE AGAINST THE MOONS

FROM THE EMPIRE

STORY BY
SUNAO YOSHIDA

ART BY
THORES SHIBAMOTO

D0111038

STORY	Sunao Yoshida
ILLUSTRATIONS	THORES Shibamoto
TRANSLATION	Anastasia Moreno
ENGLISH ADAPTATION	Jai Nitz
EDITOR	Kara Stambach
INTERIOR AND	
COVER DESIGN	Jose Macasocol, Jr.
LAYOUT ARTIST	Jennifer Carbajal
ART DIRECTOR	Anne Marie Horne
DIGITAL IMAGING MANAGER	Chris Buford
PRODUCTION MANAGER	Elisabeth Brizzi
MANAGING EDITOR	Vy Nguyen
EDITOR-IN-CHIEF	Rob Tokar
VP OF PRODUCTION	Ron Klamert
PRESIDENT AND C.O.O.	John Parker
PUBLISHER	Mike Kiley
C.E.O. & CHIEF CREATIVE OFFICER	Stuart Levy

First TOKYOPOP printing: April 2007

10 9 8 7 6 5 4 3 2 1

Printed in the USA

TRINITY BLOOD Rage Against the Moons -FROM THE EMPIRE- © 2000, 2001 Sunao Yoshida. First published in Japan in 2001 by KADOKAWA SHOTEN PUBLISHING CO., LTD., Tokyo. English translation rights arranged with KADOKAWA SHOTEN PUBLISHING CO., LTD., Tokyo through TUTTLE-MORI AGENCY, INC., Tokyo. English text copyright © 2007 TOKYOPOP Inc.

Library of Congress Cataloging-in-Publication Data
Yoshida, Sunao, d. 2005.
[Toriniti buraddo. English]
Trinity blood. Rage against the moons / story by Sunao
Yoshida ; art by Thores Shibamoto ;
  translation Anastasia Moreno.

p. cm.
Audience: age 13-23
ISBN 978-1-59816-953-9 (v. 1 : alk. paper)
I. Shibamoto, Thores. II. Moreno, Anastasia. III. Title.
PN6790.J34T67613 2007
741.5'952--dc22
2006028180

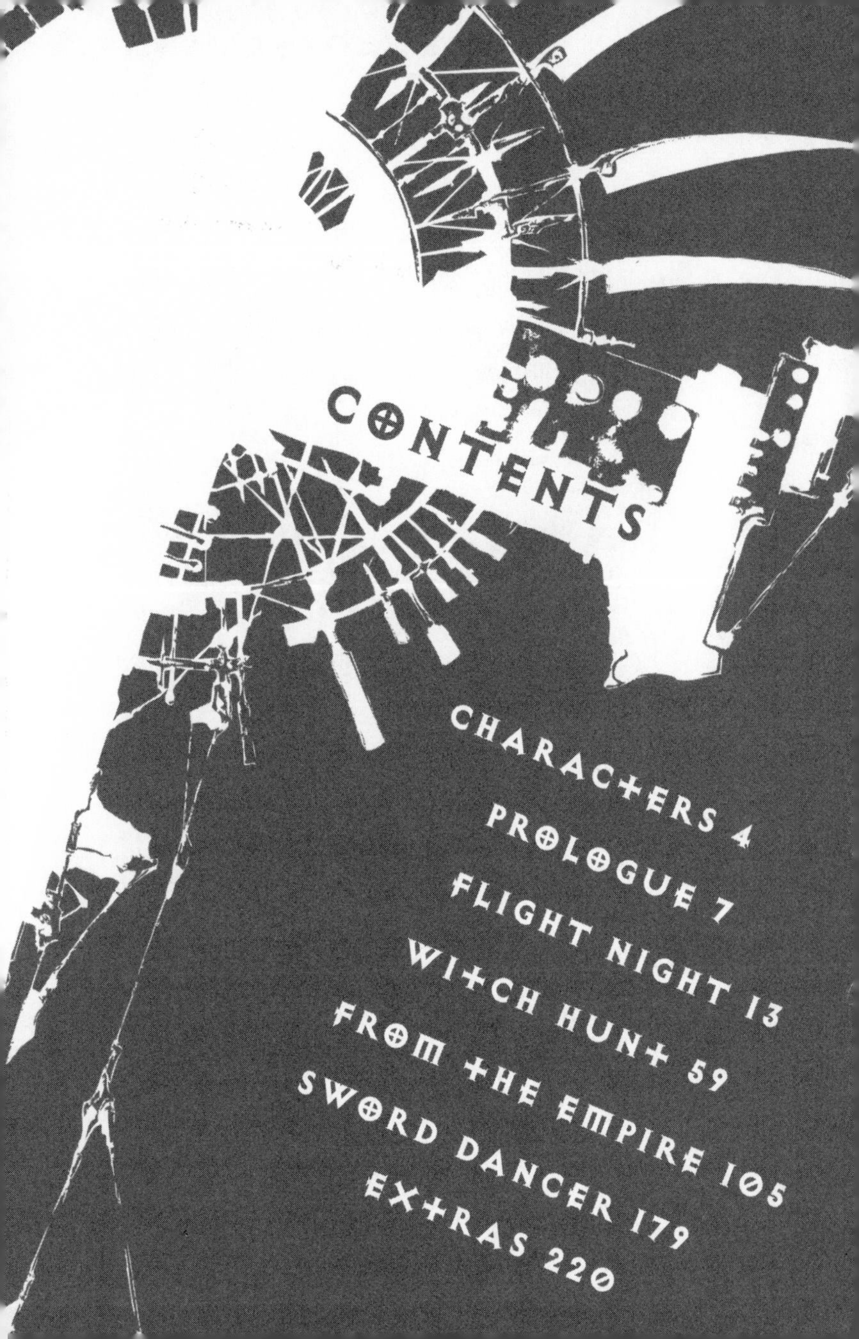

CONTENTS

THE CHARACTERS IN
TRINITY BL⊕⊕D
RAGE AGAINS+ +HE M⊕⊕NS

ABEL NIGH+R⊕AD

HUGUE DE WA++EAU

TRES IQUS

CA+ERINA SF⊕RZA

KA+E SC⊕++

ISAAK FERNAND V⊕N KAMPFER

Abel Nightroad—Oddball priest; AX Agent "Crusnik"

Tres Iqus—Android priest; AX Agent "Gunslinger"

Kate Scott—Holographic nun; AX Agent "Iron Maiden"

Hugue de Watteau—Noble priest; AX Agent "Sword Dancer"

Caterina Sforza—Cardinal & Foreign Affairs Minister

Isaak Fernand von Kampfer—Rosenkreuz Orden Officer & Inventor

JESSICA LANG

ERIS WASMAYER

ASTHAROSHE ASRAN

Jessica Lang—Stewardess of the passenger airship *Tristan*.

Eris Wasmayer—A girl kidnapped by vampires.

Astharoshe Asran—Duchess of Odessa. Undercover agent of the New Human Empire. Vampire.

PROLOGUE

The moonlight shone through the gorgeous stained glass window, making the blustery winter night seem all that much darker.

"Amen. This meal I have prepared is my body. On this holy night, I give thanks." The elderly voice was gentle; the man who spoke was reverent of his holy ritual, and his words were eloquent and full of passion.

But the eyes of the nun—her arms and legs bound to the altar and her mouth gagged—were wide with fear.

Perhaps she wouldn't have been so afraid if a mere cold-blooded murderer stood before her. After all, a murderer would only kill her. A cold-blooded murderer would at least be *human*.

"Thank you for being so patient, Sister Angelina. It's time for the Last Supper," he said somberly.

The nun gasped.

When the old man turned, moonlight reflected off the silver blade gripped in his wrinkled hand. He had used the knife countless times to slice bread for worshippers, back when he'd been mortal. But now, the knife was ragged and tarnished from his unholy touch.

" 'Take this bread, for it is my flesh.' "

He carefully cut the nun's habit from her head. The sound of the ripping fabric tore through the eerie silence. Slowly, he trailed his fingertips down her pale skin. His touch made the veins in her chest swell. Her pulse raced.

" 'Take this wine, for it is my blood.' " He sighed wistfully. "Oh, Angelina. You will become a part of me. Through my veins, your blood will live in an eternal night."

The old man flashed a wicked smile; long white fangs poked past his lips. Unable to check his bloodlust, the old man pointed the knife at Angelina's white breast. But just as he was about to slice into her heart—

A whisper came from the shadows. *"Ite missa est.* This Mass is over, Father Scott."

"What?"

Just beyond the altar stood a gentleman draped in shadows. Even a vampire's extraordinary senses could barely detect his presence. He was practically invisible to a normal human.

"Londinium priest Father Alexander Scott . . . In the name of the Father, and of the Son, and of the Holy Spirit, I am placing you under arrest for seven counts of murder and extortion of blood," the stranger said.

"Who the hell are you?"

"I beg your pardon. I come from Rome—"

It was his mistake to afford the vampire any courtesy. Instantly, the knife flew across the distance between them with near-impossible speed. The aim was true, and the knife stabbed the shadowed man squarely in the chest.

"I don't know who you are, but no one interrupts my supper!" the priest said. The elderly vampire laughed so hard, his long white robe rippled as his shoulders shook. White fangs glinted in the darkness.

The priest hadn't been a vampire for more than a month, so two suppers in one night would mark his finest feast.

"It was foolish to sneak up on the living dead, my son."

"Foolish for you to think I would fall so easily," the man replied.

"What the . . . ?" Father Scott couldn't believe his eyes.

The knife had sunk deep into the shadowed man's heart, yet there he stood, unaffected.

"I heard one of your sermons once," the stranger murmured regretfully. "You preached that humans are the only beings capable of believing in themselves. Your faith made me want to show you compassion, but . . ." the shadowed figure trailed off.

"H-how . . . ?" The elderly priest, who had traded sunlight and decency for the strength and power of immortal evil, now cowered, frozen in fear. "Are you a vampire too?"

"No. I am . . . what I am."

Suddenly, the sound of metal bending and popping split through the air. The figure stepped forward, his own priest's robe slowly absorbing the knife, until it was engulfed deep into his chest.

The vampire growled. "I'd heard of your kind, when I was still human. In Rome, at the Vatican headquarters, there was a sect of priests that kept a monster. When the Vatican had problems beyond the scope of mortal men, they sent the monster to do their bidding. Is that you?" the vampire asked.

The stranger cocked his head. "AX. Spelled out, it is the *Arcanum Cella ex Dono Dei*. My boss doesn't like scandals, you see. She wouldn't want news spreading that a priest had 'changed.' That's why I'm here."

From out of nowhere, the shadow-clad man raised a double-bladed scythe high into the air.

Father Scott glanced at the scythe and then shrieked in horror. "You're Caterina's hound! AX Agent Crusnik—!"

A whipping, winter wind drowned out his scream.

FLIGH✝ NIGH✝

Therefore, he that made them will not have mercy on them.
He that formed them will show them no favor.
—Isaiah 27:11

I

Stewardess? May I please have milk in my tea? And about twelve . . . no, thirteen sugars?" he asked.

Jessica peered back at the young man on the other side of the counter. He wore thick glasses and a plain, faded priest's robe. This poor traveler looked very out of place.

Though recent times had been hard, the observation lounge was elegant and lively. Well-dressed ladies and gentlemen chatted and chuckled, lively music played, glasses clinked, and cigar smoke hung in the air. The lounge was full of rich and gorgeous people. It was a perfect night for flying.

"Um, stewardess? Ma'am?" he asked again.

"Huh? Y-yes!" she replied.

Jessica ran a hand through her brown shoulder-length hair, forcing herself to wake from her daydream. She tied on her apron. Her smile made her youthful, freckled face light up. "Uh, did you ask for a scotch?"

"No, tea with milk. And thirteen sugars."

She blinked. "Well, if you want some sweets, we have cakes and pies, sir."

"I'm sure they're wonderful, but . . ." The priest looked into his wallet. His shoulders slumped. "I only have four dinars . . . so I'll just have some tea, please."

Even the rich children running amok in the lounge had more money than that. In fact, Jessica's pay the previous week was two thousand dinars. How did this poor priest even get on the

Tristan—the most luxurious airship that flew between Londinium and Rome?

"My job always makes me cry," he joked. "The cafeteria here charges a hundred dinars for dinner. What a rip-off! I'm so poor, one meal will clean out my bank account."

"Don't tell me you haven't eaten?" she asked.

He shrugged. "Not for about twenty hours. I was trying not to exert myself by just sleeping in my room, but I was starting to feel light-headed anyway. I thought that maybe if I raised my blood sugar a little, I could hold off until we reached Rome," he replied earnestly.

"Priests live such a hard life."

The priest took Jessica's sympathy as a compliment. He nodded as if he were praying to God. "Sometimes our jobs mean life and death for the faithful . . . So, can I have the tea and sugar now?"

She nodded. "Sure. Here you go."

"Mm. This tea tastes so smooth. It's authentic, isn't it? Not that brewed-in-a-bag stuff that leaves you—"

WHAPT!

Before the thick liquid could reach his lips for a second sip, a little child running through the lounge with a balloon bumped into the priest's elbow. The glass bonked the priest's chin. Sugary tea spilled everywhere—on his long hair, his robe, his glasses, everywhere. Meanwhile, the child tripped, fell on the floor, and started crying.

"Are you okay, little boy? Are you hurt?" Jessica asked.

She completely ignored the silver-haired priest, who stood there with tea dripping down his face. Instead, she ran to the child. Luckily, the boy was more startled than hurt.

Jessica snatched up the balloon's string. She'd given a balloon to all the children as they boarded. Returning it now, she gently hugged the boy.

"Th-thank you, miss," the boy stammered.

"You're welcome. But you need to go back to your parents. It's close to your bedtime."

"Y-yes . . . I'm sorry, Father." The boy looked sheepish.

The priest smiled, one eye visible beneath dripping wet hair. He threw his head back and laughed. "Oh, it's okay. Only a cup of tea. No problem. I'm not worried about it. Not at all."

Jessica smiled until her eyes crinkled with pleasure. "Isn't he such a nice priest? Well, you need to get to bed. Make sure you go straight to your mother."

The little boy nodded and ran off. Jessica made sure he'd safely left the lounge before she looked at the priest.

He stared at the spilled tea. He just stared and stared, his expression so remorseful.

"Father, would you like a sandwich? You don't have to pay—it'll be on the house."

He brightened. "On the house? Really? Oh, Lord, thank you, stewardess. Are you an angel? Now that I think about it, there's a picture of you in our church."

She rolled her eyes. "I'm just a stewardess."

After a short sputtering noise, an automated voice piped in through the intercom on the lunch counter.

"This is the bridge—Jessica, can you bring us our meals?"

"Yes, Captain Connely . . . Um, Father, can you hold on a minute? I'll be right back," she said.

"I'll wait as long as you ask me to, Miss . . . ?"

"Lang. I'm Jessica Lang."

"Lang?" the priest repeated. He thought for a moment. "Any relation to the airship designer, Doctor Catherine Lang?"

"Yes. She's my mother."

The priest's eyebrows shot up. "Wow. Can you fly this ship?"

"No! I'm just a stewardess. I've studied flying a little, but I'm not certified yet, since I'm a woman, you know . . ."

"There's no law stopping you from flying, Jessica. I know a woman who flies an airship . . ." He trailed off, then shook his head. "Oh, I beg your pardon. I'm Abel." The priest bowed low as he introduced himself. "Abel Nightroad—wandering priest, at your service."

The *Tristan,* at two hundred fifty yards long with six hundred thousand cubic feet of helium, was the third largest airship in the world. Only the Germanic Kingdom's *Midgaurd Gerange* and the Kingdom of Franc's *Charmaneau* surpassed it. But, its top speed of one hundred miles per hour and its luxurious passenger service put the *Tristan* in a class all its own.

The passenger airship was the Albion Kingdom's jewel of the skies.

"Here you are, Captain," Jessica said.

"Oh, thank you, dear. You know, I pilot this monster just for perks like these," Captain Connely confessed. He smelled the coffee's rich aroma. The steam moistened his neatly trimmed mustache. He sort of looked like an Albion noble.

"It's peaceful up here," she commented.

"Peaceful is good . . . We have six hours until Rome," the captain replied.

The helmsman and engineer were relaxed and in good spirits—sure signs of a quiet journey.

"Where's Deputy Roswell?" the captain asked.

Dickins, the navigator, looked around the cramped bridge to the empty seat next to the captain. "I saw Roswell down below. He didn't feel well, so he's taking a break, Captain," Dickins informed him.

"He didn't seem well back in Londinium, either," observed the captain.

"Was it something physical or personal?" asked Mr. Orson, the helmsman, raising an eyebrow.

"Probably something he ate." Dickins winked. "His wife is the nicest woman I know, but . . ."

The *Tristan's* small crew looked undermanned for such a large ship, but they were in complete control. Their confidence soothed the most skittish of fliers. And their confidence was well earned. The *Tristan's* auto-control system, designed by the genius engineer Catherine Lang, was the ship's finest feature. A "computer," a relic of a past civilization, controlled the *Tristan*. As a result, the ship needed only one-tenth the number of crew members. The revolutionary design was unparalleled.

"Mister Orson, what's this?" Jessica pointed at a control panel. "The trim is off a bit. Shouldn't you adjust it?" she asked.

"Let me see. Huh. It is. How did you know that?" he wondered. Mr. Orson looked intently at the control panel and adjusted a knob. It was quite funny to the rest of the crew.

"Why don't you let Jessica steer?" Dickins suggested.

The captain laughed. "You'd make my job easier."

Jessica blushed with embarrassment. She felt badly for showing up Mr. Orson. "I'm just a stewardess," she blurted out.

"But you applied at this company to be a helmsman, right? What a waste. Why can't they be better judges of talent?" the captain complained.

Captain Connely was known for his progressive outlook. He wanted the best crew, regardless of their gender. He figured that the job was too dangerous to let old customs get in the way of doing the best work possible. Age and gender had no bearing on his analysis. His inspiring attitude was why Jessica had applied for work on the *Tristan* in the first place.

"I'll bring that up to my superiors next time," the captain said.

"Thank you. But you don't have to do that on my account," Jessica murmured sheepishly.

"It's our duty to recommend people with real talent, Jessica."

Just then, Deputy Roswell returned. His pale face and sweaty brow were in sharp contrast to the demeanor of the cool and collected crew.

"Where've you been, Roswell?" the navigator asked. "And who is that?"

Behind Roswell, a man followed. Roswell began to stammer out an introduction when the man interrupted, "I am Alfredo, Duke of Meinz, of the Germanic Kingdom."

The duke bowed in an exaggerated fashion. The inverness he wore, an expensive overcoat complete with cape, was fastidiously tailored. He plastered a sinful grin on his young face. "Pardon my intrusion, but I told Mister Roswell that I have a passion for airships. After some convincing, he offered to let me have a look around the flight deck," the duke purred.

"Duke, I apologize, but we cannot allow you up here," the captain said politely. His tone switched from polite to scolding when he addressed Deputy Roswell. "What's wrong with you, Deputy? You know unauthorized personnel aren't allowed on deck!" The captain fumed.

The duke said tonelessly, "Sir, please don't get mad at him. It's my fault."

Jessica didn't like something about the duke's mannerisms. Instead of being noble or refined, he seemed crass and unapologetic. She thought about how grating this rich duke was, and how amiable the poor priest had been just a few minutes ago. Though he had no money, the priest seemed much richer in spirit.

Come to think of it, she didn't remember any Germanic nobles booked on the *Tristan* this night.

"My apologies, Duke, but we can't allow you on the flight deck. I'm sure you understand," the captain repeated.

"What a shame," the duke said. "I wanted to crash this baby into something big, y'know? Just on a lark."

The duke's black humor was wasted on the crew. Especially on Captain Connely, who said, "This airship has an auto-control function. Even the crew can't change the flight route . . . Hey! What are you doing?" Captain Connely asked, bewildered.

The duke slid a small metallic disc from his sleeve and dropped it into a slot on the control panel. The captain reached for the duke's arm, but it was too late.

"What have you done? What was that?"

Dickins stood up to protest, but suddenly his display screen flickered and shut down. Before he knew what was happening, the screen flooded with indecipherable text.

"Captain, the computer is denying access!" yelled Dickins.

"What did you do?!" demanded the captain. "The passengers!"

Captain Connely's thoughts veered in every direction. He was completely dumbfounded. Then the ship lunged forward, taking a steep nose-dive, and he was thrown back into reality.

"Settings for our destination have changed—altitude has dropped to minus three hundred! We're going to crash!" the helmsman yelled.

The duke merely chuckled. A thin smile stretched his lips. "That's it? Too damn easy if you ask me!"

Dickins grabbed the duke's collar and shook him violently, but that condescending smile remained permanently etched on the noble's face.

"Are you insane?! You're going to die, too!" Dickens bellowed.

"I don't think so, you filthy Terran. Death isn't in the cards for me," the duke said dryly. Beneath his smug smile, the duke's slender white fangs protruded. "I am a Methuselah! Death can't catch me!"

"Vampire—!" spat Dickins. He almost didn't get the word out, before the duke ripped his throat open.

The navigator, choking on his blood, screamed and then fell to the floor. Everyone froze in shock, staring at Dickins as he writhed in agony. It was all the time the duke needed.

Blood spurted across the flight deck. Every spare inch of the room was filled with screams of pure horror. One by one, the crew members fell victim to the duke's brutal ministrations.

Eventually, only Jessica remained.

The color drained from her face when she realized her fate would be much worse than a quick death.

"Pussycat," the blood-covered duke crooned. He was impossibly calm. It was unnerving, but not as disturbing as the predatory way he looked at Jessica. His lecherous grin revealed his fangs. "Mmmm." The duke licked his lips.

Jessica's world was spinning out of control. Were all the crew dead? She couldn't hear them howling anymore. She couldn't hear them breathing. Her heart was pounding so loudly.

She saw Roswell strewn on the floor next to her feet, his head missing. Frantically, she scanned the room for it and when she finally found it, her stomach sank. His head rested on the control panel, his face frozen in an eternal scream. Jessica's thoughts flashed to his wife for a brief moment.

The duke towered over her. "That's the guy with the nice wife, right? It really bothers you, doesn't it? What will his family think? They aren't *thinking* about anything. I already raped and killed them."

Jessica trembled with fear. She was heartbroken. It was worse than she'd thought. Alfredo's finger slipped along the opening of her top. Tears welled up in her eyes as he molested her. It was going to be *much* worse than she'd imagined.

"Stop," she said in a steely voice, but her tough exterior wasn't fooling anyone.

"You're really pretty, you know that? I think so. Girls like you are a double dip of delight. First, hot sex. Then? A hot meal."

Alfredo grabbed her breast in one hand and cupped her crotch with the other. As he did, he opened his mouth wide. Jessica arched her back exactly as he'd expected, and his fangs lined up perfectly with her neck.

"No!" Jessica whispered. She started to scream when the fangs pierced her skin, but instead, a familiar voice made her freeze.

"Miss Jessica, I was thinking . . ." The priest's gentle voice echoed from outside the open hatch. "It's against the tenants of the Church to take your generosity without offering to repay you. So I thought that maybe I could wash dishes or clean the bathroom or something," the priest said, finally stepping through the door.

Abel looked at the scene: the blood, the body parts, Jessica, and the duke. A normal man would have gone into shock at the sight of such carnage, but Abel Nightroad wasn't a normal man.

He was a clumsy man.

The vampire pulled back at the sight of the priest's robe and hissed, "Vatican!" A thin cord flew out from the under his cape.

"Vampire!" Abel shouted.

Abel slipped on the bloody floor just as a blade whizzed through the air toward his head. He landed on his butt.

BANG! Suddenly, a gunshot startled all of them.

The gun strapped on Abel's hip had accidentally gone off. The bullet ricocheted off the floor and hit a pipe on the wall behind Jessica. The pipe broke and hot steam scalded the vampire.

The duke released Jessica and covered his face. Apparently, even a vampire's eyes and face were sensitive to boiling steam. The scathing hot jet would have killed a normal human, but it just infuriated the duke.

"Miss Jessica! Over here!" Abel shouted.

The priest grabbed Jessica's elbow, turned, and ran. She looked back over her shoulder to see the blind vampire cursing and slashing at the consoles.

"You're dead, Vatican dog! You hear me? I'm gonna rip out your intestines and strangle you with them!"

III

Are you hurt?" Abel asked softly.

Jessica's eyes stared blankly out into space. "They're all dead. Th-they're all—" she stammered. Wrapping her arms around herself, she collapsed to the floor.

They'd managed to run far away from the flight deck, but she couldn't help looking around nervously. That monster was still with her, his taint still on her.

Abel could almost see her thoughts etched on her forehead. He tried to calm her down and get her to focus on the task at hand. "He won't follow us. Even a vampire will take time to heal from those wounds. What did he do to the ship's controls?"

"He said that he'd crash this ship into Rome." She sobbed. "And Mr. Dickins tried to stop him, but . . . and the captain . . ." Her words hung in the air.

Abel wanted to comfort her. He wanted to hold her close and promise her that everything would be fine. But he couldn't do that. Too much was at stake for him to waste time taking care of her.

"Calm down, Jessica," he quietly commanded.

She vomited. Abel put his arm around her heaving shoulders. He pulled her hair back and held it gently in his hands. Looking up to the ceiling as if asking God for guidance, he sighed. *What a nightmare.* The computer was compromised, a vampire terrorist was on the loose, and the bridge was in disarray. There would be full-scale panic if the passengers found out.

"What should we do, Father?" Jessica asked.

"We need to stop him."

But how? Jessica wondered. The duke had already attacked the ship's main weakness: the computer. They didn't stand a chance of saving the ship. *No one knows how a computer works. Secrets to the old technology were lost ages ago.*

"I've seen the blueprints of this ship. It has a sub-bridge, right? It's in the hangar with a messenger plane. We can control it from there."

"That's impossible," she said, wondering where he got his hands on blueprints in the first place. "The *Tristan* is on autopilot now. The manual override is extremely complicated, and there are layers of protection. We'd need to unlock those. It's all controlled by the computer."

The computer was the most mysterious of all the relics left behind from before the Armageddon. Only specialists called "programmers" could decipher the large volume of coded ones and zeroes into logic. She didn't know what the vampire had done to the system, but it would take an amateur years to figure it out.

Abel nodded. "I have an idea. We can disconnect the computer controls and pilot the ship from the sub-bridge."

She hesitated. "Technically, we could . . . but we don't have a helmsman."

Abel smiled. "You can fly this thing."

Jessica gasped. "What?" She pulled away from him. "No way! Nuh-uh! I can't!"

"Earlier tonight you told me—" Abel began, but she cut him off.

"I'm just a stewardess!" she yelled.

His smile dropped. "So you're just going to let us crash?"

Jessica didn't have time to refute his point. They both heard footsteps running down the hall.

"Oh no!" Jessica nearly fainted.

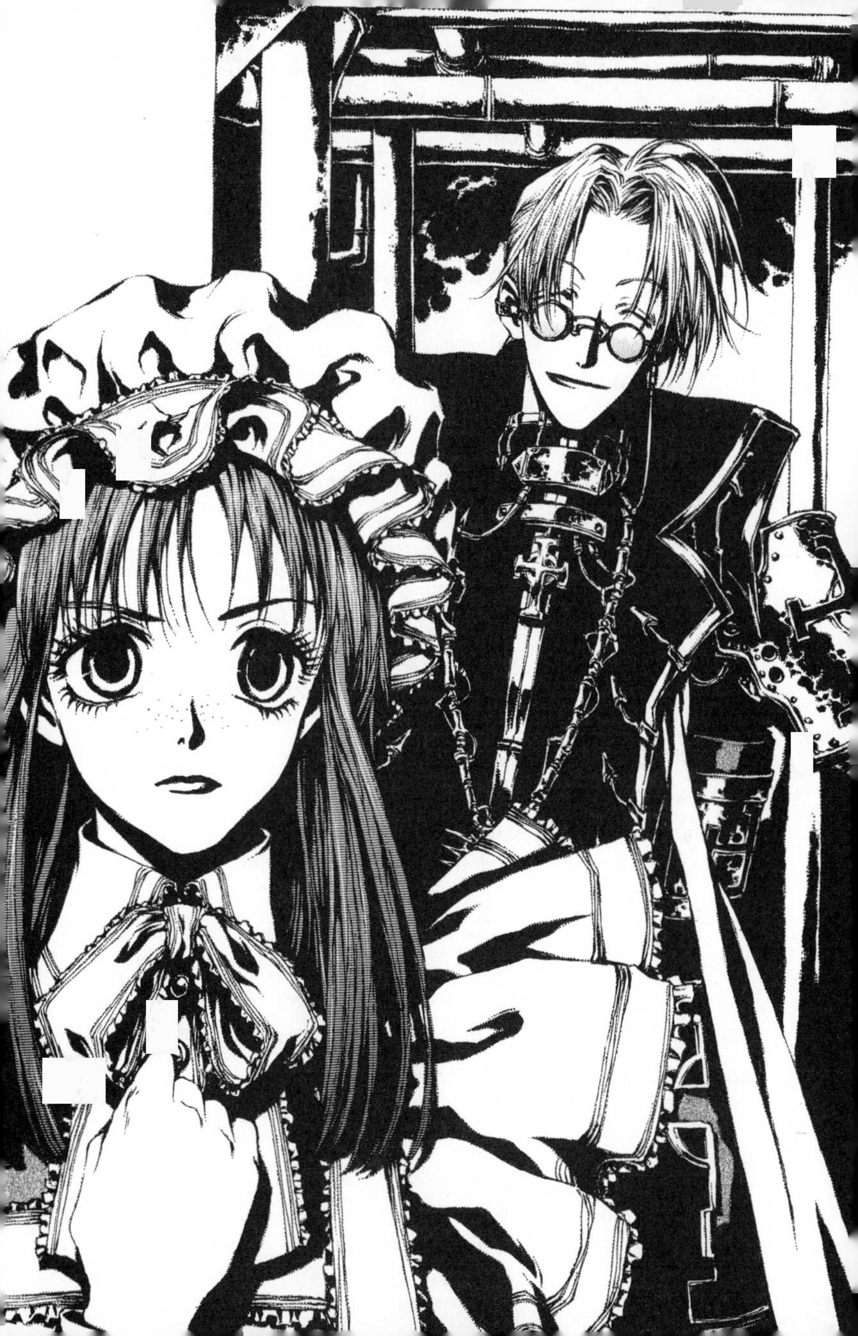

"It's not him; the footsteps are too light," said Abel.

The little boy who'd had the red balloon suddenly rounded the corner. He looked lost and scared. He ran to Jessica, about to burst into tears.

Immediately, Jessica pulled herself together. "Oh dear. Come here. Are you lost?"

The boy nodded vigorously.

"Didn't I tell you to go back to your mother?" she asked.

"Mommy's down there," the boy said.

"What?" Dread filled Jessica's heart.

The boy sniffled and continued. "Mommy's in Rome. Daddy and I are going to see her."

"You'll see her soon," Jessica reassured him.

The boy smiled at her confidence and calmed down.

Jessica bit her lip. *This boy won't see his mother. He'll probably die. And not just him.* All the other passengers, including herself, and the airship that her own mother worked so hard to build, would most likely be destroyed.

"Father?" she whispered.

"Yes, Jessica?"

Abel smiled knowingly at the light in Jessica's eyes. Her shock and despair had given way to strong determination—she was ready now.

"We have to get this boy back to his father," Jessica said.

"And then?"

She shrugged. "And then we do what we need to do."

"Yes, *we* will. I like that kind of spirit in humans—" Abel stopped in mid-sentence and shook his head.

✝

The radio transmission that came in at 01:40 A.M. was loud and clear, even if the message itself was warped: *The Vatican must release all vampire prisoners within the next hour or we will destroy Rome.* It was insane.

In the castle of San Angelo, the Messenger Angel Hall, otherwise known as the Vatican war room, was hectic—people shouted and papers scattered about. Everyone important was there: Head Priest of Papal Security, Deacon of Transportation, and even the pope's sister, Foreign Affairs Minister. They'd all been roused from their beds, but none of them seemed the least bit tired.

The skinny young boy at the head of the table, on the other hand, looked like he was about to doze off.

"We've received preliminary intelligence from Department of Inquisition!" shouted an aide.

"Duke of Meinz, Alfredo, vampire—wanted for sixty-seven counts of murder and diablerie," read Head Priest of General Security. "How did that murderous thug get onboard the *Tristan?* How did he slip past security?" he asked, fixing accusatory eyes on the deacon of Transportation.

"Your Holiness, are you awake yet?" asked Minister of Foreign Affairs. The beautiful woman clad in cardinal red smiled as she looked down at a boy.

The youth, his mouth stretched wide with an enormous yawn, collected himself enough to look up in surprise. Alessandro XVIII, three hundred ninety-ninth Pope, looked very much like a child kept up past his bedtime rather than the ruler of the Vatican, the most powerful authority in the world.

"Sorry, elder sister. I fell asleep," he said sheepishly.

"You shouldn't be up for this, Alec. We can handle it," she said soothingly. The Duchess of Milan, Minister of Foreign Affairs Cardinal Caterina Sforza, looked warmly at Alec from behind her monocle. "You should be resting."

He blinked rapidly. "I'm okay. What's going on?"

"It's bad." Her calm expression downplayed the gravity of the matter. The situation inside the airship was still unclear, and there was nothing the Vatican could do at this point. "Worst-case scenario? We give into their demands," said Caterina.

The young pope frowned. "It would prevent bloodshed." Alessandro thought for a moment in silence. Then he nodded vigorously and tapped the edge of the table. "Yes. We will release the prisoners," he stated flatly.

A deep baritone voice raised an emphatic objection. "We cannot do that, Your Holiness," the voice boomed.

"Elder brother?"

"Cardinal Medici," Caterina nodded, acknowledging the man who'd spoken.

The siblings exchanged cold glances. There was no love between them, and everyone in the room knew it.

Secretary of Vatican Papal Doctrine Francesco di Medici was a large, intimidating man. His body was more suited for war than the papacy. He removed his mortarboard and stiffly bowed to the pope. "I have returned from my visit to the Assisi Air Force Base."

"Wh-when d-did you get here, elder brother? I thought you were away until next w-week," the boy stammered.

"I have just arrived. I also heard about the incident on the *Tristan*. Well, Caterina?" Cardinal Medici asked.

The blonde beauty stiffened at his rebuking tone.

"You should know better than to advise the pope to give in to the demands of vampire terrorists. He will become a weakling in their eyes—a puppet that they can hold hostage any time their desire fancies it. You should be ashamed of yourself!" he barked.

"Bro . . . My apologies; I meant Cardinal Medici," she replied to her half brother. "What are we to do? The *Tristan* is from Albion, full of Albion civilians. The deadline for signing the Albion peace treaty is next week. We can ill afford a problem in the peace negotiations. Matters with Albion must be handled delicately," she reasoned.

"The Vatican does *not* negotiate with terrorists. Especially *vampire* terrorists!" Cardinal Medici scoffed. "Your Holiness, we must not submit to their demands. Forbid them from entering Vatican airspace."

"Will they obey our orders?" the pope wondered. The room fell silent and the young inexperienced pope felt everyone's stares burrowing into him. He swallowed thickly. "If they were the kind of people who would obey our orders, they wouldn't have hijacked the airship in the first place, would they? I'm sorry. It's no use."

"It would probably be a waste of breath," confirmed Caterina.

"Then what do we do?" the timid pope asked.

"We give them a warning. If they invade our airspace, we shoot them down. It's quite simple," said Cardinal Medici. His words fell like a ton of bricks.

Caterina shouted in protest. "Are you out of your mind, Cardinal Medici?! I've just said the *Tristan* is Albion's ship!"

"*Beate sumpto qi miribundum in Domino.* Happiness is to die in the name of God," he replied.

The priests instantly backed up Cardinal Medici:

"The Vatican enforces God's will, and we will shed blood to protect his holy doctrines!" shouted one.

"God will not bow down before terror!" yelled the cardinal.

Caterina looked at every man in the room, but saw only bloodthirsty fools. They desperately wanted to slaughter in the name of God. And they would, unless the pope forbade it.

Her older half brother was very charismatic, but he often wielded the Vatican's authority too forcefully. *Times have changed; the public won't support unnecessary violence. The people are no longer a mindless flock of sheep.* Caterina's train of thought was interrupted by a deacon.

"Cardinal, ma'am, we have urgent information," the deacon said hurriedly. He quickly handed a list of names to Caterina.

"The *Tristan's* passenger roster? Good work, Deacon."

Caterina's heart sank as she saw the long list of names. Each one was a brother, sister, father, mother, or child. They were all in grave danger.

When she spotted one name in particular, her demeanor instantly changed. "Deacon? Are you sure this is correct?" she asked carefully.

"Yes, ma'am. It's been confirmed by three different sources," he said. "It's accurate information, ma'am. There is a Crusnik on the *Tristan*. The evil abomination was on his way back to the Vatican after arresting Father Scott."

"Watch your tone, Deacon. That 'evil abomination' is one of my most loyal agents. In fact, call in all AX agents. Which ones are readily available?"

The deacon bowed. "My apologies, Cardinal. Gunslinger and *Iron Maiden* are standing by. They can be in contact with the *Tristan* in four hours."

"Those two can support the Crusnik and safely secure the *Tristan*. It's going to be bloody . . ." She paused, taking a deep breath. "Casualties are acceptable as long as they remain less than fifty percent. Anything more than that will ruin our chances of peace with Albion."

Caterina looked around the room. The hall continued to swirl with activity. The matters they handled were life-or-death in nature, but the bigger picture was at stake. A treaty with Albion could mean a lasting peace, an end to all bloodshed between the two nations. While she silently weighed the global ramifications of the Vatican's actions, she looked at her brothers.

Cardinal Medici barked orders. He looked like a madman who could barely control himself. Meanwhile, poor Alec seemed completely overwhelmed. He was just a boy, even if he was Pope. The Lord saw fit to make him Pope, and she would do all she could to help him in this trying time. Having her most trusted AX agent aboard the *Tristan* was an absolute godsend.

God's dove is flying to Rome.

"*Laudare nomune Domini*. Praise the Lord," she whispered.

IV

CREEEAK. CRUUUUUNK THOOM!

The floor collapsed.

There was nothing they could do. In vain, they scrambled to hold on to something, but they were sucked down the ship's pipes. It wasn't a long fall, but it was frightening and disorienting.

They rose, groggy and off-balance.

"Owww. Father, are you okay?" Jessica asked. She couldn't see anyone in the small gray room. She craned her neck and peered into the darkness. Then she felt it. "Father? Where are y—eek!"

Something moved under her skirt. Jessica jumped up and screamed at the top of her lungs.

Abel, his eyes rolled back in his head, lay beneath her. He looked half hurt . . . and yet more than a little satisfied. She must've sat right on his face when they'd landed.

"Father, are you all right? Please don't be dead."

"It hurt, but it felt good," he mumbled. "Where am I? Who are you? What smells so good?"

Abel continued to babble on for a few moments before he could shake the cobwebs from his addled mind.

Jessica, fearing he'd had a concussion, tried to snap him out of it. "We're on the sub-bridge. The floor panels were rusted and they gave out. Are you feeling all right?"

"I had a dream. There were angels, but they were wearing pink instead of white. And they smelled sweet, like perfume . . ."

Abel's voice trailed off when his mind caught up with what he was saying. He snapped his mouth shut and blushed.

Jessica stared coldly at the squirming priest. She took great care to chastely adjust her dress. "There has to be an electrical switch around here somewhere," she said, looking anywhere but at Abel. "Ah. Here it is."

"So, this is the hangar for the messenger plane. We can leave any time we need to."

Jessica ignored the priest and moved to the computer switchboard. She knew which knobs and levers needed to be flipped for manual flight, so she began typing in the command sequence. After a short time, the makeshift bridge was up and running. The computer booted up, but the display revealed a blinking cursor, nothing more.

"I don't know what this is, but there should be information on here, a prompt to enter a password or something. Right now, we're completely locked out," she said.

"Is that so? Let me see," said the priest.

"It's no use. Only a programmer can—" Jessica stopped in mid-sentence.

At the console, the priest was typing furiously. She thought he'd lost his mind and was just banging away at the keyboard like a madman. She didn't have time for such foolishness.

"Father! Quit wasting our time with that nonsense! We need to find another way to divert the ship."

He simply replied, "I know what I'm doing."

The computer screen filled with strange characters—green letters and numbers, rushing rapidly down the monitor. After a while, Jessica began to see patterns in the chaos. Bits of words, pieces of code, and specific breaks in character sequences started to add up.

"Got it," said the priest. He punched a large key, and then raised both fists in triumph.

The console beeped at them and began to whir. A moment later, the switchboard lights changed from green to blue. Jessica knew this meant they'd gone from autopilot to manual mode.

"Who are you really, Father?"

"I'm the guy who's going to cover you while you fly this ship to safety." The priest straightened his robe and looked around. "I worked my miracle; now it's your turn. You need to keep this ship from crashing at all costs. That's going to be the easy part. Landing's the hard part. You stay here; I'm going to look for our friend from the flight deck."

"Isn't that dangerous?" she asked.

He searched her face. "It's dangerous to let him find you here—I won't let that happen. I'll do my job, you do yours."

"Uh . . ."

"Yes, Jessica?"

She didn't know what she was trying to say. She couldn't sort out the tangled mess of her emotions. Finally, she settled for "Be careful."

"Thank you." The priest's sharp blue eyes seemed to soften whenever he looked at her. "I'll be back; holler if you have any problems."

Abel had barely finished his sentence when he was flung across the room. He flew through a pane of glass; the shards shredded his face and clothes. Most human beings would have been decapitated, but Abel merely lay there, limp as a rag doll.

Jessica turned to see the vampire before her. She wanted to scream, but her throat closed up. She stood in silence for what felt like forever.

As if savoring her terror, Alfredo, Duke of Meinz, took a long time before he spoke.

"You'll holler before I'm through. I promise you that."

V

Abel landed flat on his stomach—or what was left of his stomach. The vampire's punch had shattered his ribcage. He felt his organs spilling out beneath him, along with copious amounts of his blood.

He felt so cold.

"I thought you weren't foolish enough to try something like this." The duke laughed. "Did you think I wouldn't find you? Are you really that stupid?"

All hope Jessica once had now faded. Abel was dead, and she was about to be violated. *No, it'll be worse than mere rape,* she thought. The vampire would probably sexually torture her, and then take his sweet time draining her dry. Crippled with fear, she fell to her knees.

"Not so fast!" the duke said, chuckling. He smacked his lips, chewing on a wad of tobacco. "While you'll spend plenty of time on your knees tonight, it won't be until after I've knocked your teeth out. But business comes before pleasure." The vampire gave her a feral smile.

Jessica tried to back away, but she couldn't. She was helpless, enthralled. She couldn't even brace herself.

"Be patient, honey. I know you'll break easy, but I want to do it spectacularly. I'm going to do things to you that humankind hasn't seen in a thousand years. Horrible things. Wonderful things. You'll beg for more and you'll beg for death—at the same time."

The duke pulled out the metallic disk that he'd used on the bridge and held it up high.

"What is that?" Jessica asked, curious despite her fear.

"I think it's the master code for the computer. But, you wanna know a secret? I really don't know what it is. They told me to put it in the computer and push a few buttons. Amazing that something so small can bring down this big ship, huh?"

Startled, the duke suddenly jerked back.

"No," came the eerie whisper. Thin fingers grabbed Alfredo's leg.

Jessica gaped. *It's the priest! How is he still alive?*

"Please, there are over a hundred people on this ship," the priest ground out.

"I don't give a damn about those worthless people!" screamed the duke. Alfredo kicked Abel squarely in the temple. The force of the blow sent the priest skidding into a wall of machines. He lay sprawled on the floor, broken. Jessica heard the wet *thud* as his innards smeared along the ground. Her eyes welled up with tears.

"I'm a Methuselah. A vampire! We are the highest beings on Earth! You are like cattle! I will use you for food and wear your skin when I'm done with you!"

"No . . . you . . . you're also human," whispered the priest, moments from death.

"Shut up and die, you stupid cow," growled the vampire. Duke Alfredo typed away on the keyboard. "I'm almost done here, pussycat," he said over his shoulder to Jessica. "After this, I'm gonna kill you 'til you love me."

She didn't know how she'd gotten a pipe, and she surely didn't know where she'd found the strength to swing it—but she aimed for the vampire's head and gave it her best shot. He blocked the pipe with his bare hand, not even bothering to look up from the keyboard. She knew then that he saw her as a mere toy, weak and helpless—something to play with, break, and discard.

Alfredo used the pipe's momentum against her, twisting her arm behind her without so much as looking at her. With a flick of his wrist, he threw Jessica into the wall. She crumpled to the floor.

"Je-Jessica!" the priest choked out.

"Holy crap! Did I kill her?" The duke laughed, shrugging. He continued to chew his tobacco. "Oh well, her corpse will be warm for a few more minutes, at least."

He started whistling a funeral march while he typed, trying not to let his mood turn sour. Sex with a corpse was one thing, but he didn't want to drink a dead person's blood. It always tasted terrible. He spit out his tobacco.

"What is that?" Abel asked.

The black blob the vampire spit out wasn't tobacco after all. It was a piece of red rubber. It was . . .

"A balloon . . . ?" Abel whispered in disbelief.

"That? Oh, I got it from a little boy," remarked the duke. He continued to type without glancing at the balloon or Abel. "I found him on my way here. I was looking for you, of course. I knew you'd come to the sub-bridge, but I needed to feed before I could make it here. The boy's blood helped me heal faster. He tasted good. His blood was thick, smooth . . . and it flowed until the very end. Exquisite, really."

What happened next unfolded faster than the vampire could see, faster than he could hear, faster than he could smell. He was, for the first time in his life, caught completely unaware. The duke was thrown to the ground with terrific force. He fell, squealing like a pig, "What?!"

A normal human would have broken every limb. The duke was merely dazed by the impact. He raised his head for the briefest second, taking in the priest who stood before him.

"Duke Alfredo, you've gone too far," Abel said.

Shadows painted the priest's face. Even the light from the two moons outside couldn't penetrate the absolutely black halo that now engulfed the priest. His robe was soaked with his own blood. The duke couldn't comprehend how the priest could still be alive, much less find the strength to fight a Methuselah.

"I regret that I cannot forgive you . . . unless you're willing to repent," said the priest.

"Forgive? Repent?" asked the duke. "You're insane. I am above your human concept of sin!" Duke Alfredo pulled himself up off the floor and hissed at Abel. "Your cow-god holds no judgment over my soul. You are no more than a dinner buffet to me. And your faith is useless," spat out the duke.

"He would forgive you, but . . ." The priest's eyes glowed a horrible red that would turn the stomach of the bravest men. "Even if He could show you mercy . . . I cannot."

"Tell your cow-god all about it when you get to cow-heaven!"

Alfredo jabbed a middle finger at Abel, attempting to poke out his eye. The duke didn't think the priest would blabber on about God and redemption if he were blind. He greatly anticipated the satisfying squish his finger would make when he dug into Abel's eyeball, eye socket, and brains.

But . . . nothing.

"Impossible," the duke whispered.

Abel had caught the vampire's arm. *It takes the strength of ten humans to hold back the arm of a Methuselah. Who is this human?* He tried to free his arm from the priest's grip, but he couldn't. That wasn't the only surprise in store for the duke.

"Nanomachine Crusnik 02 forty percent limited performance—authorized," Abel murmured.

"Agaaah!" screamed the duke. Agony shot through him and he yanked his arm back. He staggered, in the worst pain he'd ever known.

A chain was now wrapped around his wrist. The links of chain ate at his flesh like they had minds of their own. Small bloody geysers sprayed from his arm. Bone and flesh dripped off in chunks all around him. The chain was shredding his arm to pieces.

"My haaaaaaand!" the duke screeched.

"Hurts, doesn't it?" the priest asked coolly. His eyes were a red darker than blood. Fangs suddenly protruded from his lips. "Doesn't it? Are you suffering? The people you killed endured far more pain. I won't kill you now. Instead, I will do God's will. I'll only make you bear one hundredth of the pain the people you've murdered had to bear."

The horrible sound of popping flesh filled the room. It was sickening. It wasn't the duke, however. Abel's right hand and arm were splitting open. From inside the gaping hole, a sharp spike poked through. It pulsated.

It was a mouth.

The mouth began eating Alfredo's right fist.

"Y-You're . . ." the duke stammered. "Wh-what are you? You're not human."

"You compared humans to cattle, didn't you? Haven't you ever thought about this: Humans eat cows. Vampires eat humans. Maybe there's something eats vampires," the priest whispered. Abel's lips curled up to reveal his fangs. "I am a Crusnik. A vampire's vampire, if you will."

"Bullshit!" Alfredo hollered in disbelief. "I am a Methuselah. All the living creatures of Earth are mere fodder for us. We rule by the divine right of kings! We were ancient when your world was young! I am a god! Die, you Vatican dog!"

Hidden in the duke's belt was a microfilament knife. The edge had been sharpened down to a hair; it could cut through anything.

It now sprung up like a snake. Abel guarded his face with his left hand, but the blade moved at supersonic speeds and sliced off his left arm. A column of blood spurted up to the ceiling.

"Mortal weakling. 'Vampire's vampire,' huh?"

Bleeding and in horrible pain, Abel took a knee.

Duke Alfredo snickered at him. "You'll pay for the indignities I've endured. What are you? A human augmented by drugs and technology? No matter. You'll pay all the same. I'm going to cut off your other arm, and then both your legs. Then, while you bleed to death, I'll rape the girl and drink her blood right in front of you. You'll cry for me. Oh yes, you will."

Abel didn't bat an eye. He just picked up his left arm from the floor. A sucking noise echoed around the room. The mouth on Abel's arm moved again. It started to eat the rest of the severed left arm: fingers to palm, palm to wrist, wrist to forearm.

"You're eating yourself," observed the duke. "Disgusting."

Abel's body began to change shape. A new arm started growing out of the wound. It was a regeneration of sorts, but it was happening impossibly fast. New flesh grew out, piece by piece; first the fingers, then the palm, wrist, and forearm. Eventually, the biceps and shoulder snapped into place.

He wasn't human, and he sure as hell wasn't a vampire. The duke knew this. He started to back away. His mission to crash the *Tristan* didn't seem so important now. Before him stood something beyond his experience, something even more cursed than a vampire.

The priest cocked his head. "I will ask you one question, a question that might save your life." His simultaneous consumption and regeneration was now complete. But that was the least of his powers, the duke sensed. Seemingly from thin air, a double-bladed scythe appeared in Abel's hands. "Who are you working for?"

Duke Alfredo didn't answer. He just ran. He bolted as fast as his vampire powers allowed. He scrambled to an outer access door and fled the ship itself, scurrying to the top of the helium balloon.

The duke's mind raced. *Will I have to jump?*

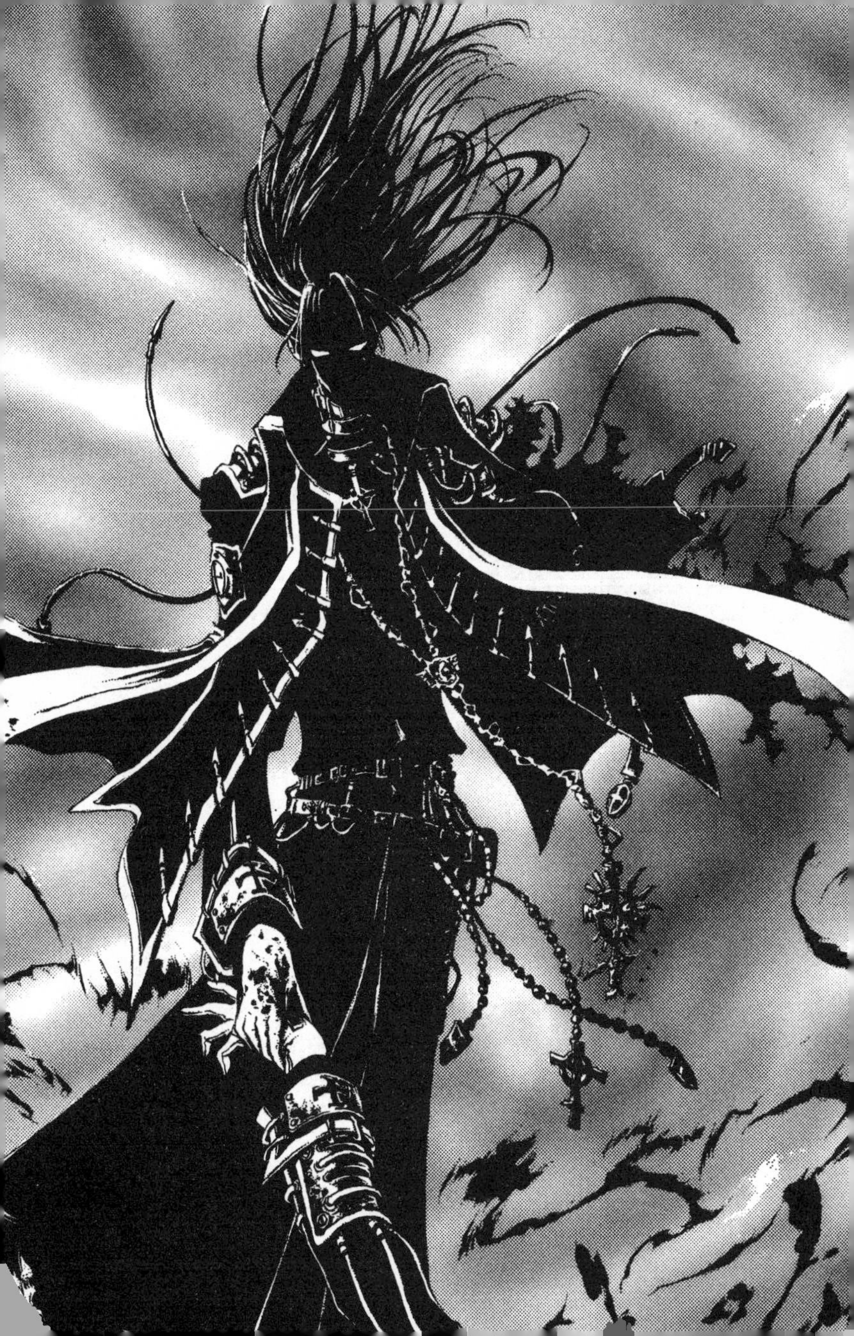

He didn't have to think about it for long. Abel suddenly appeared in front of him. *How could anyone have outrun me?*

"It's useless. You cannot escape me." The vampire could just barely hear the priest's voice above the whipping wind.

Where does he come from? What is he? The duke almost didn't care anymore.

The air around them was freezing but the priest just stood there, not even a warm cloud of breath trailing his lips.

Alfredo whimpered, afraid for his life. *What is he?!*

The twin moons glowed down on them. Finally, Abel broke the silence. "What are you afraid of, Duke? Aren't you safe at the top of the food chain?"

The duke screamed as he charged forward, but it was merely a feint. Duke Alfredo swung his belt at the priest and then turned to run. His plan was semisuccessful. His legs ran in one direction . . . but his torso fell in the other.

His lower body ran a few steps before it stumbled and flopped over. His hands reached out for his thighs, but found only empty air. "Help me. Please help me," the vampire begged.

Abel's red eyes looked down to the mortally wounded vampire. "How does it feel to be cattle?"

As his guts poured out, Alfredo tried to scoot away. He was terrified. Rational thought was impossible.

"Speak," ordered the priest.

The duke was compelled to answer. He just blurted out information that he'd once sworn to keep secret.

"Rosenkreuz Orden . . ."

Duke Alfredo felt something squeeze his heart. He was certain that it was the priest. But when he looked, it was his *own* hand tearing into his chest. He was crushing his own heart.

"What's going on?" he squeaked.

His hand acted on its own and pulled out his heart. *What the hell is happening?*

"Oh no! Pre-hypnotism!" the duke whispered, watching himself die.

The priest swung down his scythe to sever the heart from Alfredo's hand, but in vain. The mangled organ was already crushed like a grape. The duke gurgled off his immortal coil.

Abel knelt before the fallen vampire, closed the corpse's eyes, and whispered, *"Calpa perrenis aelito ora tuor nominare.* Your sins are eternal. But I will not pray for the dead."

The priest rose. The rosary between his fingers clanked, swaying in the intense wind. "I don't like this one bit," he said as he looked at the burst heart. "Not one bit."

VI

Jessica rolled over in bed. *What a terrible nightmare!* She'd dreamed the *Tristan* had been hijacked and she'd teamed up with a weird priest to try and stop the nefarious terrorist plot.

Why is there sheet metal in my bed?

"Hello!" shouted the priest.

Jessica's bed started shaking. Then she realized it wasn't her bed at all. Then she realized that no one was steering the ship.

"Jessica! Please wake up! The helm, the helm!"

Jessica came to and leapt up. "I've got it! I've got it!" she screamed.

"Thank God!" the priest cried.

Jessica grabbed the controls and the shaking stopped. The ship righted itself and continued to fly smoothly.

"Well done, helmsman. Uh, helmswoman. Um, Jessica," the priest babbled.

"Where's the vampire, Father?" Jessica asked nervously.

"He was thrown out the access door when the ship started shaking. It was a miracle."

She knew he was lying, but there was too much to do right now to question him. She picked up the radio. "Rome Air Traffic Control, please respond. This is the *Tristan,* Albion Airline, flight 007."

"*Tristan,* what is the status of the hijacker? Are you okay?" the control tower responded instantly.

Jessica thought about the priest's lie. It was all she had to go on. "The hijacker was accidentally thrown from the aircraft. Request guidance from air traffic control. We have several casualties, including the pilots."

"Sorry *Tristan,* we can't provide a vector for flight! You need to take evasive action!"

"What?!" Jessica didn't understand what was going on.

The instruments indicated that they were about three or four hours from Rome.

"We are not authorized to continue transmission. Please just take evasive action! God be with you. Rome Tower, out."

"Hello? Hello?!" Jessica screamed.

"What's wrong?" Abel asked.

"The control tower stopped responding even though they know we don't have a pilot!"

The *Tristan's* beeping radar cut Jessica short. She shrugged her shoulders. "The radar must be broken. According to this, three objects are approaching at six hundred miles per hour. Even airplanes don't fly that fast."

Abel ran to the radar to see for himself. "Cut off the engine!"

"Eh?"

"Cut off the engine and drop altitude! Now!" he screamed.

Jessica didn't understand Abel's sudden expertise in piloting aircraft, but she did as he commanded. She cut the engine, and let out some of the helium from the balloon. The craft descended.

"More, more! Get us almost on the ground!" Abel shouted.

"I've already let out too much helium. What's going on? You're freaking out over a radar glitch."

"It's no glitch," he responded. Abel frantically looked back and forth between the map and the radar screen. "Missiles. The objects are missiles, a lost technology of the ancient civilization. The rumors about tests at Assisi were true."

Jessica didn't understand a word of what he was saying, so Abel continued to explain. "Missiles can track the heat trails of engines, even after they are turned off. We're trying to lose them by dipping low and cutting our exhaust. The missiles might hit the ground. That is, before we do."

"How is that possible?" Jessica asked in disbelief.

He wanted her to fly the *Tristan* low to dodge these missiles. He was asking her to put them in guaranteed danger to avoid possible danger. Jessica started to protest.

"Just get us lower to the ground. I have an idea," the priest said before darting off.

"Where are you going?" she asked after him.

The *Tristan* entered a thick fog that hovered just above a deep ravine. Jessica consulted the map carefully and steered the ship hard to starboard. A mountain suddenly came into view on the port side. Luckily, Jessica was savvy enough to avoid it and kept the ship in one piece.

One of the approaching objects fell off the radar, just as they dipped low. So, the priest wasn't crazy after all.

"Come on! We've still got some work to do!" Jessica yelled at the *Tristan*.

As if responding, the *Tristan's* huge body shivered and sped up. The ship swung past the treacherous terrain as if an ace pilot were at the helm. A whole regiment of guardian angels must have been looking after her.

"Good Lord," Jessica gasped.

The sub-bridge mirrors showed a ball of light approaching on the horizon just behind the *Tristan*. It was like a rocket-propelled snake, winding through the clouds.

"You won't beat me," Jessica declared.

She put her whole body weight on the wheel and spun it. She bit her lip so hard that it bled, then screamed, "I won't lose to that thing!"

The tips of the wings dipped low and scraped along the tree line, snapping off the tops of tall pines. The trees burst into flames as they fell. Luckily, the missile couldn't make the turn and crashed into the terrain.

But there was still one left.

"We're not going fast enough for another turn! I can't dodge the next one!"

"It's okay. Thanks for buying me time," came Abel's voice from over the intercom.

The missile was too close. It was going to hit them any second.

Just then, the rear hatch of the sub-bridge opened and the messenger aircraft dropped out of the back, its engines already running. It bobbed in the air, then spun to the side. The ignition fired, leaving a trail of burning jet fuel. The missile adjusted course, latching onto roaring engines even hotter than the *Tristan*.

Jessica gasped.

The explosion stole her breath. *What did the priest do? Did he pilot that plane just to lure the missiles away?* She stared at the remnants of the airborne explosion. "Oh no, Father! You did that just to save us." She wept; her tiny frame wracked with sobs.

Then she stopped suddenly. Remembering his words, she gripped the wheel firmly in her grasp. "I'll do my job; you've done yours." Her hot tears fell onto the console. "I never even gave him the sandwich," she realized.

"That's why I'm extremely hungry right now," he whispered.

Jessica turned to see the priest leaning against the console, holding his ribs.

"Father! You're alive?"

"It took a lot of energy to get that plane off and still jump out before the missile reached us. I really *am* hungry."

Jessica plowed into him, hugging him tightly. She buried her face into his chest and cried.

Abel fell backward, exhausted but happy. "Um, you're choking me, Jessica. And the ship is going to crash."

Like before, Jessica straightened up and chastely collected herself. She took the wheel, restarted the *Tristan's* engines, and gained altitude.

Abel put his hand on her shoulder and gently stroked her hair. "You did your job well."

"As you did yours, Father."

Abel's expression darkened. The *Tristan* was safe, but he had some unfinished business. He pulled the piece of balloon from his coat pocket. *Somewhere on this ship, a father is looking for his son.*

Reluctantly, Abel removed his hand from Jessica's shoulder. "Take care of flying the ship. I need to go check on the other passengers."

Jessica exchanged longing glances with him. Then she remembered that she was staring deeply into the eyes of a *priest*. She turned her head, embarrassed by her own thoughts.

Just then: *BEEP BEEP BEEP!*

The radar showed an unidentified object hurtling toward the *Tristan*.

"The third missile!" Jessica exclaimed. "It's back! We can't dodge it; we can't cut the engines at this angle!"

"Duck!" Abel yelled as he grabbed Jessica to him. They fell to the floor just as the missile detonated. It blew out the windows of the sub-bridge and sent shards of glass raining down all around them. The *Tristan* heaved to one side.

Jessica screamed, but she couldn't hear her own voice over the deafening explosion. She clung to the blood-soaked priest as they tumbled across the floor. Jessica said a prayer, thinking this was the last moment of her life. She prayed for Abel, and silently told her mother she was sorry.

Then she heard Abel's voice, but he sounded like he was talking into a can. His words were garbled; she had to read his lips.

"Let go of me, please," Abel said.

"What?" Jessica asked. She could barely hear the sound of her own voice.

The smell of gunpowder and smoke at least proved that she was still alive. She looked around, seeing that the sub-bridge's floor had tilted, and she was now on top of Abel.

"Are you okay, Jessica?" he asked, sincerely worried.

"What happened?"

"Tristan, can you hear us?" asked a soft female voice over the intercom. "This is the Vatican Papal State AX Air Battleship *Iron Maiden.* We will guide you to Rome. Please follow our directions."

"What the hell does that mean?" Jessica asked, before she remembered she was in the company of a priest. She couldn't face him she was so embarrassed, so she kept her gaze on the window. The clouds parted and the largest airship she'd ever seen jutted through. "Lord Almighty, it's so huge!" she exclaimed.

It was bigger than life. It made the *Tristan* look like a toy.

The battleship passed between the *Tristan* and the twin moons, momentarily blotting out the sky. Jessica could just barely make out its design. The ship, with beautiful curves of sleek steel, had a distinct Roman cross painted on its side.

"Good evening, Sister Kate. Sorry to bother you. Again." Abel chuckled.

"I'm used to it, Father Nightroad. But I didn't take care of the missiles. It was Gunslinger. He says you owe him one," replied the radio.

"Tell him I'll buy him a drink," Abel joked.

"That's a negative, Abel. *Iron Maiden,* over and out," replied the radio.

Jessica heard a faint giggle over the radio before it fell silent. She cast a sideways glance at Abel.

"Those are my friends from work," he said nonchalantly.

Abel finally had time to take stock of his own appearance. His robe was soaked in blood: his, the duke's, and the crew's. One sleeve was missing from where he'd lost an arm. All in all, he didn't resemble an ordinary priest.

He looked at Jessica's wide eyes and smiled. "We're safe now, Jessica. Nothing in the world can get within ten thousand miles of us," Abel reassured her.

It was hard for Jessica to believe it. She looked out the window again, marveling at the *Iron Maiden*. It was just too big to comprehend. Between the duke and the missiles, she was still quite unnerved.

The clouds thinned and the first light of dawn broke over the horizon. For a moment, a strange calm came over her. "Beautiful" was the only word she could muster. *Beautiful to behold. Beautiful to be alive.*

The windows had been blown out, so the smell of wet earth and flowers wafted on the breeze. The skies gradually turned golden.

Jessica held a firm grip on the helm and rolled the words over in her head a few times before she spoke. "Abel? Can I ask you something?" Jessica turned to look into his eyes, ready to pour out her feelings, wanting to see his face when she did.

But he was nowhere to be found. She looked around the sub-bridge, but the only other thing she could see was her shadow.

"Father?" she asked.

✝

Palazzio Spada buzzed with activity in the predawn light. No one had slept the previous night.

Cardinal Caterina Sforza was taking a break after working the whole night through. The streets below her office bustled with laborers and office workers; the noise comforted her. She wasn't alone in her crusade for peace and safety. She knew that everyone down below would give their all for the Vatican. She smiled and sipped her tea.

"Renewal of Albion Trade Agreement Passes" read the morning headline. The Vatican Public Affairs office had outdone themselves. There was no mention of the hijacking in the news at all that week. The deaths of the crew were attributed to a bizarre food poisoning. That also explained the erratic flying to the passengers. All in all, it was wrapped up rather neatly thanks to her agents.

Cardinal Caterina gazed down at the newspapers through her monocle, resting her teacup gently to the side. She delicately wiped the corners of her mouth and carefully folded her napkin before replacing it on her desk. Inhaling the tea's pleasant aroma, she closed her eyes.

"Something's different about the tea. Hmm . . . Chamomile, lemon grass, honey . . . and peppermint?"

"A wonderful guess, Cardinal Sforza. I added the peppermint and a drop of quince," replied the hologram on the cardinal's desk. The holographic image was of an elderly nun with a mole on her cheek. She was pleasant in the most comforting way. Her smile could calm a raging bull.

"I noticed that you were tired lately, so I made a recipe that would be gentle for your throat. Does it suit your tastes?" the hologram asked.

"Quite delightful, Sister Kate. Thank you," the cardinal replied.

Cardinal Caterina neatly folded the newspaper when she was finished. She drained the last of her tea and rested her chin in her hand. Last week's events weighed heavily on the cardinal's mind. It was a victory for the young pope, but that didn't make it sting any less.

"Sister Kate, about the hijacking, when can I expect a detailed analysis report?" the cardinal asked.

"Intel is putting the finishing touches on the in-flight report as we speak. In fact, I expect it within the hour. The background report is taking longer than expected. I'm sorry for that," the hologram apologized.

It had been a week since the hijacking. The incident and the cover up operations were kept quiet, but as far as solving the actual crime was concerned, there were too many unanswered questions. The cardinal's head felt very heavy.

It was daunting: motive, accomplices, access to the ship, the disc, the murder of one of the crew member's family, all of it. The lone hijacker had committed suicide when he was asked who put him up to the crime. There was too much going on; the plot ran too deep. Were the terrorist's demands real or a sham?

Caterina mulled it over again and again. The Vatican was the most powerful human organization on the planet. So many people looked to them for safety and support. She needed answers in the worst way. The hologram spoke again and broke Caterina's train of thought.

"We have confirmed the hijacker boarded the *Tristan* at the supply port in Matheliah Airport. Yesterday, Father Nightroad went there to investigate. We'll have his report shortly."

"They haven't left any other evidence for us. Why would Matheliah be any different?" the cardinal asked rhetorically.

It felt like they were chasing a ghost. There were so many intangible factors at work. The plot was so big that there had to be something, somewhere she could latch on to.

All they really had was the hijacker's confession before his suicide. Alfredo, Duke of Meinz, had named the Rosenkreuz Orden as his employers.

Is this some kind of ruse as well? It can't be the Rosenkreuz Orden. They've been gone for ten years, and they never had the will or means to pull off something like hijacking the Tristan.

At this point, Cardinal Caterina Sforza was positively swimming in doubt.

WI✝CH HUN✝

Thou shalt not suffer a witch to live.
—Exodus 22:18

This is horrible." Abel Nightroad sighed.

He pushed his thick round glasses higher up his pointed nose, oblivious to the beautiful night. Outside, a nightingale perched somewhere in the bushes, singing softly. The sweet sound, coupled with the symphony of crickets and bullfrogs, made the evening, lit by glowing twin moons, all the more peaceful and pleasant.

Abel noticed none of it.

He stood inside a small building. It had been a bar or a meeting hall in another life, but tonight it was a slaughterhouse. There were bodies scattered everywhere, many ripped to shreds. Streaks of blood covered the walls from floor to ceiling. The red liquid dripped down into dark puddles and began to coagulate.

The smell was almost unbearable. Pieces of internal organs littered the room, coating everything with the sick scent of fecal waste. The remains were still warm; this crime was recent. The squish of Abel's boots over the paste of human flesh drowned out the nightingale altogether.

"Why wasn't I here sooner?" he asked himself.

A sudden splash in a blood puddle turned Abel's head. He spun on his heel. "Who are you?"

An odd figure crouched behind an overturned table. The stranger approached Abel, blood and guts squishing with each awkward step. It was slightly hunched over, holding something in its hands. Unafraid, Able started to address the stranger directly, but his words morphed into a shocked gasp.

Moonlight illuminated the stranger. It was no man, but instead a grotesque vampire. Covered from head to toe in gore, jagged fangs jutting at various angles, the creature held a woman's blood-soaked head in its hand.

There was something wrong with it, even for a vampire.

"Grrarraraahahha!" The creature leapt at Abel.

Abel braced himself for the attack. He set his back foot on a relatively clean patch of floor to avoid slipping. The vampire sailed through the air quite easily. Abel flexed the muscles in his arms and back, preparing for his counterstrike.

BOOM!

A deafening blast and a flash of sharp light interrupted the silent combat. The vampire skittered to the ground in a heap. Furious, it tried to scream, but its innards frothed up in its mouth. Its arms and legs flailed as if pulled by separate strings. The large vampire spat and writhed down in the muck. As it attempted to stand, it was suddenly riddled with bullets. The vampire's extremities exploded. Fingers and toes flew in every direction. The vampire seized and spasmed.

Abel covered his face and ducked. His eardrums were ringing, but he was otherwise unhurt. He knew well that only one thing in the world could be so skilled with a firearm. He couldn't hear the footsteps, but he could feel them. They were rhythmic: clack, clack, clack . . . almost mechanical, heavy.

Abel finally looked up. "Father Tres."

"Affirmative," replied the electronic monotonous voice.

A seemingly young priest came down the second level stairs. His hair was neatly trimmed to match modern fashion, but his handsome face registered zero emotion. He held one of the world's largest personal handguns, the Jericho M13, with its thirteen-millimeter barrel still seeping smoke.

"Why are you here, Tres? I thought you were investigating the orphanage kidnappings. How'd that turn out?" Abel asked earnestly.

The younger priest offered no response.

Vatican Papal State AX Patrol Priest Tres Iqus, just stood there, staring blankly. After a moment of silence, he pointed his gun to the floor and shot twice.

BOOM! BOOM!

Abel jolted, almost slipping on a piece of liver. "What are you thinking, Tres?!" he screamed. Looking down, he could see the squirming remains of the mutilated vampire attempting to regenerate.

"I didn't kill him. I have some questions for him. Why are you here, Father Nightroad? Is this in connection with the *Tristan* incident?"

Abel collected himself while Tres replaced his pistol magazine.

"Yes. Duke Alfredo belonged to a group called the Fleur du Mal. They had used this place as a safe house in the past. Looks like I was too late. Lots of human casualties."

"These corpses are not humans. They're vampires," Tres replied.

"What? Why? They killed each other? They killed themselves? Wh-what happened?" Abel stammered.

"Unable to answer. Not enough data," Tres replied.

The young priest craned his neck toward the second floor. His expression did not change.

"The kidnapped orphans were already killed for food. I cannot interrogate dead bodies," Tres informed Abel coldly.

"Good Lord." Abel looked at the floor and crossed himself.

Tres moved swiftly around Abel. His gun was pointed forward as he silenty scanned the darkness.

After a few seconds, Abel heard it. But surely no one had lived through the carnage. "What is it, Tres?" he asked.

"Quiet." Tres gestured with his gun. "Over there."

Beneath the wine cellar door came the sound of rustling clothes.

"There were about twenty members of Fleur du Mal, right?" Abel asked.

"Affirmative. I estimate there to be at least twelve left. I am going in," Tres said.

BOOM! BOOM!

Tres blew the cellar door off its hinges. Splintered wood flew in every direction, but it didn't bother Tres. He moved swiftly into the darkness and ran down the stairs. The laser sights from his M13 cut through the darkness. He soon found a target. It didn't take Tres long to draw a bead and prepare to fire. But Abel grabbed his arm before the hammer fell.

BOOM!

A bullet rent a hole in the ceiling.

"Tres! Wait!" Abel hollered. "It's a child!"

Sure enough, a small blonde girl sat in the cellar. Tears streamed down her cheeks. Her big brown eyes were full of sorrow.

The girl had no idea how lucky she'd been. Tres never missed.

I

Name and age?" Abel asked.

"Eris Wasmayer. Seventeen."

"Seventeen? Didn't you say you were eighteen yesterday?" he asked incredulously.

"You shouldn't question a woman's age," she said coyly.

"Eris, can you try to be serious?" Abel sighed.

"But I'm bored," she groaned.

Eris plopped down on the bed and folded her legs. She stuck out her bottom lip and showed Abel her profile so he could easily see her pout.

If not for her bratty attitude, she would have been pretty. Her skin was clear and her bobbed haircut was quite fashionable. Still, she was terribly childish. Then again, with her short hair and no makeup, she looked like a fourteen-year-old.

Ten days ago, Eris couldn't speak. She was in such terrible shock after the incident at the vampire safe house that she had to be brought to this bunker for medical treatment and intense questioning. But now that she'd recovered, she couldn't take the situation seriously.

Funny how things change.

"I've been locked up in the bunker for days now, Father. Nothing to do for entertainment, no contact with the outside world. Then when you come back to see me, you only bring more paperwork. How many times do you need to get my side of the story?" she whined.

"Honestly! It's because you always *change* your story, Eris. I'd like to be more sympathetic, but you have to understand, I have a job to do. I have to take this to my boss, and my boss is no pushover when it comes to inconsistent facts."

Eris nodded. The priest had been nothing but nice to her since saving her from Tres Iqus' bullet. She was in the bunker for her own safety, she knew. She also knew she wasn't making things any easier on Abel.

"I'm sorry, Father. Being a priest must be difficult," she said.

"Yes, it is rough. Listen to me; my boss can be really scary. She's not the kind of person who takes disappointment well. She has plenty on her mind, and I don't want to compound her problems simply because I can't get a girl's story straight. Understand?" Abel implored.

"Tell me about your boss. Is she cute?" Eris teased.

"I'm the one asking questions here. Please cooperate. Please?" he begged.

Eris chuckled to herself when she saw the serious look on the priest's face. She loved to tease him. She was so isolated, and in order to feel wanted, her only option was to get him to keep returning.

"I'll make you a deal. I'll cooperate. But you have to get me some food from outside," she quipped.

"I can't take you outside. Not yet," he replied.

"Then go buy me something. Do that, and I'll answer your questions. The food here really sucks. I want to eat something more . . . human," she said.

"Done," he replied.

The food there did suck. He knew that. It was as bland as the walls of the bunker. It would be an easy trade-off. And it was much better than getting the evil eye from his monocle-wearing boss.

"What would you like? You name it," he said gleefully.

"I want a Gateau Chocola and Marron Glace," she said without missing a beat.

"Roger. Gateau Chocola and Marron Glace."

She might as well have asked for caviar on a golden plate. Gateau Chocola was the most expensive chocolate cake in Rome, and Marron Glace were rare glazed Spanish chestnuts. Combined, they'd cost Abel a year's salary.

Abel checked his wallet as he left the room. He looked at Eris and back to his wallet. He repeated the process. Several times. Finally Eris couldn't take it anymore.

"What is it?" she demanded.

"How about a fresh bread roll?" he responded.

She threw the pillow at the priest, then threw herself across the bed. Looking up at the ceiling, she growled, "I guess I was asking for too much when I asked for the simple pleasures of home. Just buy whatever. Anything is better than what they serve here."

"Excellent, I'm off!" Abel bounded for the door.

WHAM!

The door swung open suddenly and whacked Abel right in the nose. It sent him to the floor faster than a punch. He grabbed his nose and closed his watering eyes tight. *Boy does that hurt.*

"Hi, Tres," Abel piped from behind his bleeding nose.

"Father Nightroad?" Tres asked aloud, looking down at him expressionlessly. Tres was put together flawlessly; his robe hung exactly like it was supposed to; everything about him was tailor-made. Abel could even call him handsome, but at the moment, he smelled like gunpowder, which wasn't all that attractive.

"Didn't your mother teach you to knock before you enter a lady's room?" Abel asked.

"Negative. There is no time," Tres replied. Moving mechanically, Father Tres Iqus threw a stack of papers on the bed. "Sister Kate contacted me. We have a new place for the girl. Our orders are to clear her out of this room immediately."

"A new place?" Abel asked.

Eris visibly brightened. It was the first tingle of hope she'd felt for several days.

Abel, on the other hand, was obviously concerned. He pulled bloody tissues out his nose and examined the bright red stains. *Eris is at the center of several conspiracies. Any place crazy enough to take her in at this point is begging for trouble.*

"Saint Rochelle Convent will take her in. Sister Kate went through personal channels for this," Tres informed.

"We owe her one." Abel nodded. "Saint Rochelle Convent has great facilities, and its staff is top notch. That is, unless you don't want to leave the bunker, Eris."

"When do we leave for Rome?" she asked without pause.

"Tonight," Tres replied.

"Tonight?" Abel asked incredulously.

He wasn't comfortable with moving Eris—not without time for proper security preparations. If vampires wanted her dead, a hasty exit would only help their cause.

"A nun from the convent will meet you tonight at Central Station. Father Nightroad, you are responsible for escorting her there," Tres informed them.

"Where will you be, Tres?" Abel asked.

"I'll be interrogating at the hospital." Tres turned to leave the room but looked back over his shoulder at Abel. "The vampire from the safe house has regenerated enough to be questioned. I will continue my investigation there."

Eris glared at the stiff priest as he left the room. "I don't like him," she declared. "He isn't very nice to you."

"He's all business," Abel replied. "Besides, he actually *has* business to attend to. My investigation is at a dead end."

Abel considered what he'd just said. His leads looked bleak, but there was always something to go on. And sometimes, small leads cracked open a huge case. He mentally reviewed his notes and the timeline. The *Tristan* hijacker, Duke Alfredo, was confirmed to have boarded the craft at Matheliah Supply Airport. He was a part of Fleur du Mal, a radical vampire sect in the countryside. They were small-time, disorganized fanatics; they couldn't have possibly staged such a large-scale terrorist attack on their own. The Fleur du Mal safe house was destroyed in a horrible bloodbath where he and Tres had found Eris. She was his only link to the hijacking . . . that wasn't a corpse. There had to be something he was missing.

Abel pulled out his notepad again.

"We don't have much time, so let's finish this report. First, about your age . . ."

11

He's doing well. Too well, I suppose. We're suppressing his recovery rate with holy water," the doctor explained to Tres.

They rode a secure elevator up to the hospital's lockdown ward. No one came in or out without passing several security checkpoints. Not that any checkpoint in the world could stop Tres Iqus.

"We've cut his doses of holy water per your instructions. He should be able to talk in the next few minutes," the doctor went on.

"Affirmative." Tres nodded, then went silent again.

They were at Saint Simon General Hospital—a Vatican hospital located in the south suburb of Matheliah City. Normal patients were treated on the first six floors, but the highest floor had quarantine rooms reserved for Church use. It wasn't pleasant. The icy air conditioning blasted continuously and the lights were dim. It felt like a tomb. Tres wasn't bothered by it, of course. He never felt any weakness or emotion.

"I will start my interrogation at once. Prepare the room. Bring me the autopsy reports of the other vampires," Tres commanded.

"Nothing much to report. The autopsies show bite marks that clearly match this vampire's teeth pattern. The claw marks match his fingernails. It's an open and shut case—other than the motive for why he attacked his own kind," the doctor stated.

"That is what I am here to find out. Any other results I should know about?" Tres asked.

"There was one . . ." the doctor started, but then his eyes went wide with shock.

A nurse stumbled out into the hallway. She dug her fingers into the doctor's arms and gasped for air. She looked horrible.

"What's wrong?!" the doctor yelled.

"D–dead . . ." the nurse stammered. "H–he had no pulse . . ."

"What? Who? The vampire?" The doctor continued to fire off questions, but Tres was already moving.

He smashed through the metal door and looked at the bed. It was empty except for a cross-shaped bloodstain. The chains and cuffs were sprawled out on the floor. They looked like dead snakes. Blood dripped from the ceiling onto the sheets.

Tres looked up.

"My God!" the doctor screamed.

It was the vampire from the safe house. Someone had crucified him by nailing his wrists and ankles to the ceiling; a stake pierced through his heart. His eyes bulged, and his discolored tongue lolled out of his mouth.

"No pulse?" Tres asked quietly.

"Who let this happen? Get the chief of staff down here now!" the doctor yelled.

"No pulse," Tres repeated. "He'd never had one."

Tres tossed the doctor aside and burst back into the hallway. His movements were so fast, most hospital personnel registered him as a blur.

He pulled out his pistol and pointed in the nurse's direction. He had her in his sights for a split second, but she was gone by the time he squeezed the trigger. The hammer fell and a thunderous roar sent everyone ducking for cover.

THOOM!

A head-sized chunk was blown out of a wall behind the security desk. The nurse dodged again and slid into the elevator just before the doors closed. Tres caught up, only to find the elevator descending.

He moved to the bulletproof window and aimed his gun. "Everyone find cover," he instructed.

He didn't have to say it twice.

The glass was designed to not only withstand bullets, but to redirect them. He wouldn't be able to blast the window out. The concrete, however, wasn't as resilient. Nine shots exploded out of the pistol. The heat and sonic fury forced everyone to screw their eyes shut and cover their ears. A cloud of rubble and rebar flew through the air. Tres would have coughed if he'd had lungs.

He reared back and kicked the window. It cracked, then shattered, leaving a huge hole in the wall.

"Call the guards at the front desk," Tres ordered, even though the gun blasts had deafened everyone.

He walked through the hole he'd created.

Tres freefell seven stories. He landed on his feet, his boots crushing the concrete sidewalk into powder. The unexpected impact created mass panic. Hospital patrons outside scattered. Tres took no notice. He strode back into the hospital, reloading magazines with mechanical efficiency. Unlike the people outside, the patients in the lobby were confused, frozen in place. Tres nonchalantly walked past them, ignoring their stares.

Just then, the nurse from the lockdown ward rounded a corner.

Tres raised his pistol, prepared to turn the waiting room into a shooting gallery, but the nurse was faster than he'd anticipated.

She plucked an unlucky child from the motionless crowd. The child's mother held fast to her little girl's arms. The child kicked and screamed. None of it seemed to faze the nurse. From out of nowhere, she produced a shotgun and aimed it at the girl's temple, but the kid jerked around so much, the nurse couldn't get a clear shot.

Instead, she focused on Tres. "Don't even think about it, Vatican dog. If you—"

BOOM!

Tres' pistol clicked and a round split the air. It hit the nurse in the chest and sent her flying. It was timed perfectly. The mother and child both dropped to the floor as the nurse reared back with the force of the bullet. She hit the wall behind her with a thud, a smoking fist-sized hole in her chest.

Tres strode past the shocked mother and child. He noticed that they both had a thin layer of gloss on their hands and arms from when they had wrestled the nurse.

"UV protection gel?" Tres asked the slumping vampire. "Are you Fleur du Mal?"

The vampire spat at him.

Tres lifted the Methuselah by the neck, taking a good look at the protective sheen on the nurse's skin. UV gel could completely block ultraviolet radiation from the sun. While wearing it, a vampire could walk around in normal society, unnoticed. Humans had banned the substance years ago, and only the Vatican had any in stock these days.

"Ten days ago at the safe house, why the slaughter? What are you trying to hide?" Tres asked tonelessly.

The vampire tried to laugh at him, but ended up gurgling on her own blood. She smiled mockingly and showed Tres her fangs. "Die, Vatican dog," she whispered.

BOOM!

A gunshot silenced her laughter. The vampire had lost a hand. She squirmed in Tres' steely grip, but no matter how much she struggled, she could not free herself.

"I will heal you and wound you, again and again, for the rest of eternity. You will find no peace or rest as long as you withhold information from me," Tres threatened. He dug his fingers into the vampire's exposed chest cavity.

The vampire tried to scream, but the pain was so intense she couldn't make a sound.

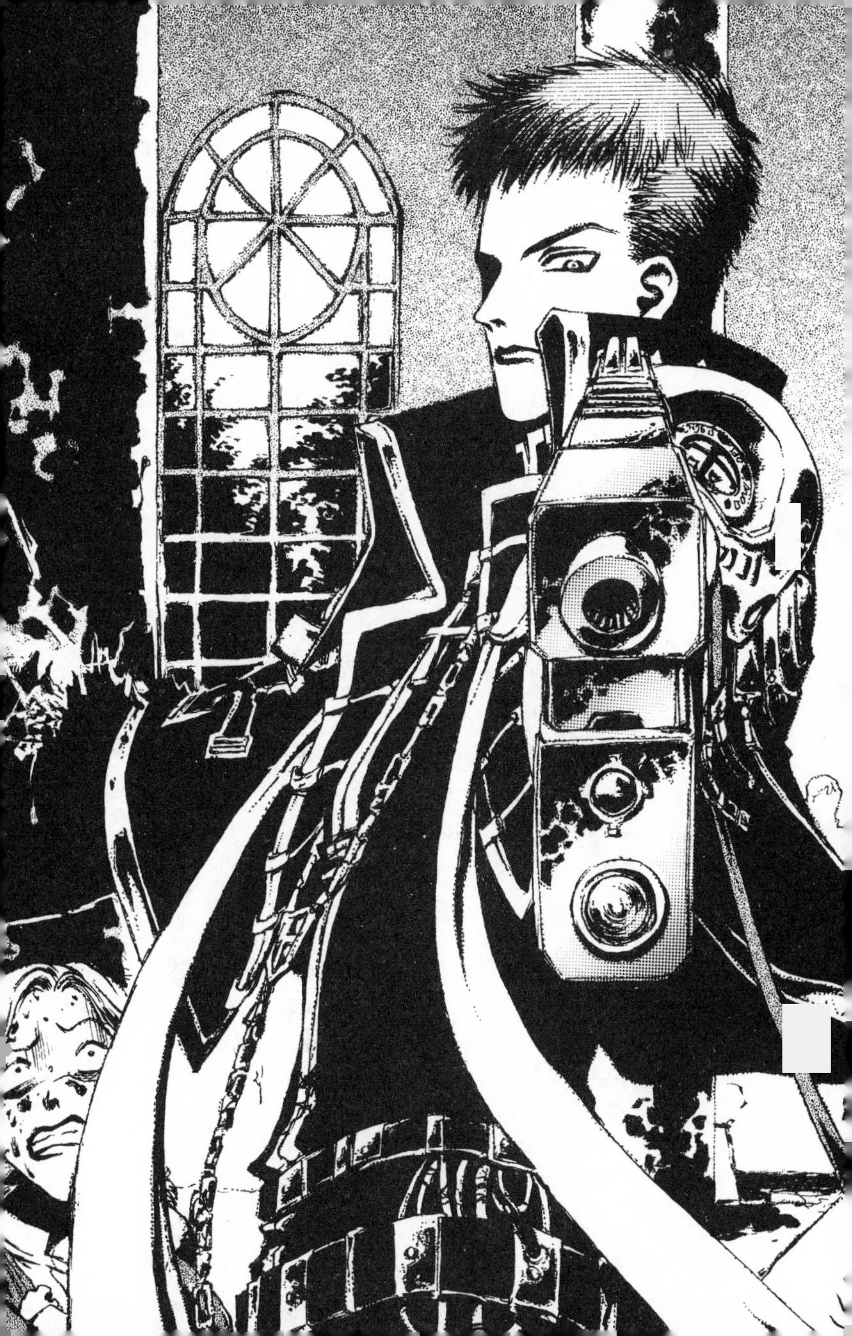

"You can end this by talking," Tres explained calmly. He sank another finger into the creature's chest.

The nurse gurgled blood and nodded. Then she spoke in hushed tones. Tres listened carefully, noting every word.

Tres threw the vampire to the side and shot her several times. He thought about keeping her alive for further interrogation, but that hadn't worked out very well for AX recently.

Tres reloaded his pistol as he walked through the silent crowd. They instantly parted for him, looking as frightened as children waking from a nightmare. The silence was broken by the sound of a potted plant smashing against the tiled floor.

"You bastard!" the mother yelled at him.

Tres turned to her and cocked his head.

"You could have killed me! You could have killed *my daughter!*" she screamed.

"Shut up!" another patient told the hysterical woman. "Or he'll kill you now."

The crowd tried to pull her away from the priest, but no one could contain the mother's fury. "Was it worth it? Huh? Was it worth it to nearly kill me and my child? Is that how you serve your God? With reckless bullets?! Have you no soul?" she shrieked.

Tres' expression didn't change.

According to Tres' internal simulation system, shooting had been the best option. Any other actions would have resulted in up to nine innocent deaths. The girl would have been taken hostage and killed in any alternative scenario. But he knew that explaining his actions would only make things worse; humans didn't see the world the way he did.

"No soul? Affirmative," he said.

Tres moved so fast that the patients could only make out a streak of color rushing past them. He scooped up the mother and her daughter in one swift movement. A bullet tore into the arm that Tres had wrapped around the baby. Reddish black oil squirted out of him as he wheeled around and drew his firearm.

The young mother didn't take her eyes off the priest. Blue and white sparks shot out of him. His artificial skin was sliced open as the round that was supposed to kill her daughter stuck in his plastic muscle.

While he covered the mother and daughter, Tres pointed his M13 toward the elevator. There sat the vampire, attempting to fire one more round with her last ounce of strength.

BOOM!

Tres Iqus fired a shot that blasted the vampire's head off.

"I am Hercules Tres Iqus, Vatican Papal State AX Agent HC-III X. I am Gunslinger," he explained as he put the mother and child down gently. "I am not a human, so I have no soul. I am a machine."

77

III

This is where our paths part ways, Eris," Abel said grandiosely. It was after sundown, but Central Station still bustled with travelers coming to and from the city.

"Sister Louise will escort you the rest of the way. Please don't treat her like you've treated me," he joked.

"It's very nice to meet you, Eris," Sister Louise said politely.

Eris shook the young nun's hand and smiled cordially. Then she turned and looked back over her shoulder at Abel. The nun seemed pleasant enough, but Eris was worried about losing her valiant protector. She gave him a pleading look that would have put a lost puppy to shame.

"I still have some work to do, Eris. You'll be safe and sound with the nuns. Just be your charming self, and they'll come to enjoy your company the way I do," he said, barely able to keep the sarcasm from his tone.

Eris playfully kicked him in the shin. Abel wasn't hurt, but he feigned it for her ego's sake. She ignored the priest and asked, "Are there any bathrooms here?"

"There are bathrooms on the train, Eris," Abel replied.

"I can't go while moving," she explained earnestly.

The priest looked at the pouting girl and sighed in defeat. "Same old Eris. Sister Louise, the train comes at ten past eight, platform number five. We'll be back in time to board. I saw the bathrooms over there," Abel said.

"We'll be back? Why are *we* going?" Eris asked in a bratty tone of voice.

"We're going together so you don't get into any trouble. Sister Louise, would you be so kind as to wait for us? Thank you," Abel said, grabbing Eris' arm.

Abel pushed her through the crowd. The lobby was lively. Hotel shuttles picked up customers, kids shined shoes for a few coins, and vendors of every type tried to peddle their wares. Abel and Eris paused in front of a kiosk that sold children's toys and trinkets. Abel picked out a key chain that caught his eye and bought it from the vendor, despite his limited funds.

"Here you are, my dear," he said.

"I can have it?" she asked.

It was a small black cat figurine. He put the keychain on her bag and patted her arm. "A going-away present. You like cats, right?" he asked.

"I love cats! Thank you," she said genuinely.

"You're welcome." He smiled.

Eris put her arm around the priest as they walked through the station; Abel was positively beaming.

"Have you ever had a cat?" he asked, trying to make small talk.

"I used to have lots of cats and kittens," she said. "Back when my real mom and dad were still alive."

The priest's smile faded for a moment.

Eris thought about her words and tried to play it off before the mood got too sullen. "It's okay. It happened a long time ago," she reassured him.

Abel's smile faded completely and he paused to look at Eris.

"Mom and Dad . . . committed suicide," she said quickly.

Abel's expression was one of sadness and compassion.

"It was a double suicide, but I guess you could say that *I* killed them," she went on.

Now Abel was confused. *It was a suicide, right?* He didn't ask any of the questions running through his mind, but just kept pace with the girl as they wound their way through the crowded station.

"I'm sorry," he said awkwardly.

"I said it's all right. I'm okay. Don't worry about it," she said. She flashed a playful smile at Abel. "I'm not the type to get hung up on the past."

"You're a stronger person than I am, Eris," Abel said honestly.

"The world is full of bad stuff and bad people. And sometimes good people get caught up in the mix. It isn't fair; it's just life. If you think about it too much, you'll go crazy. I try and stay positive and not worry until I absolutely have to. If I constantly fretted, someone would take advantage of me for sure."

"Sorry," was all Abel could think to say.

"You're alone in this world. Even when the people you care about are around," Eris said, glaring harshly.

Abel looked on in dismay. "You're not alone, Eris. You've got me," he said.

"What do you mean by that?" she asked.

"The whole world isn't against you, and you're not alone. Not with me by your side," he responded.

"Are you hitting on me?" she asked.

"Huh? Wh-what?" he stammered. Abel turned pale as his stomach twisted into knots. His words were misconstrued in the most embarrassing way possible. "No. Uh, no. I'm, uh, I'm, uh, I'm a priest. Uh. I'm not allowed to hit on anyone. I don't hit on anyone. Uh." He stammered on and on.

"Oh, how boring." She winked.

Suddenly, Eris grabbed the tall priest by the shoulders and pulled him close, until his face was right in front of hers. She leaned in for a kiss. "I've really enjoyed our time together. I've decided I quite like you," she said. "But . . ."

"But?" Abel asked.

"I'm sorry," Eris said as she closed her eyes and pressed her lips against Abel's cheek.

Abel's world went black . . .

✝

"Ungh," Abel groaned.

He didn't know where he was, what time it was, or how he got there. It took him several moments to stand up; his legs didn't want to cooperate.

The room's light was dim, but Abel felt his way around until his eyes adjusted. Eventually, he made out a steel door in a strange hallway. *Where am I?*

He tried to clear his throat and speak, but no decipherable sound came out. That had him worried. He couldn't remember a thing. The steel door seemed familiar, but he couldn't place it. Something really horrible must have happened, but everything was so hazy, he couldn't think straight.

Tiny skylights illuminated the hallway. The sky above was black, but faint moonlight filtered in. Suddenly, the floor below him lit up with white light.

Abel's heart pounded. His instincts told him to run, but there was nowhere to go.

The white light below his feet morphed into a brilliant cobalt blue ball. It transformed into a beautiful planet. White wisps of clouds slowly swirled around mixtures of browns and greens.

He looked up at the steel door and took a deep breath. Something inside him was aching to come out. His head began to hurt, and a feeling of panic washed over him once more. Deep in the recesses of his mind, his past had been carefully shut away. Now, something broke the lock on his memories.

Abel placed his hands on the steel door, noting its unusual warmth, and opened it. The white light gave way to an infinite blackness.

"Hi, Abel. You're late," a voice said.

In the darkness, Abel could just barely make out a tall man who now turned to face him. His face was totally unfamiliar, but Abel felt like he somehow knew this man who had light blond hair and a boyish smile.

Then the smell of stagnant blood caught up to him.

The blond man had something in his hand. "You should be pleased. The negative element was eliminated." He held up something for Abel to see. The rotting odor grew stronger. "Now there is no one to disrupt our plan. The traitor is no longer alive."

The blond man was holding a female's head. She had a beautiful face, but now she was grotesque.

Abel screamed in anguish, but no sound escaped him . . .

"Are you all right, Father?" asked the train attendant.

Abel blinked at a pudgy train station worker. The employee looked at the priest with concern. "Are you not feeling well?"

"Not feeling well?" Abel repeated.

Sweat beaded his forehead. He was confused and nauseated.

Someone bumped Abel with their luggage. The sounds of the train station filled Abel's ears, and blurry reality finally came back into focus.

"Your face is very pale," the train attendant stated. "Shall I take you to the first aid center?"

"Ah, no, I'm okay. Sorry," Abel said.

He shook his head violently, clearing the cobwebs. He remembered Eris kissing him, and then the world went black. *Where is Eris?*

"Eris?!" he shouted.

The train attendant jumped.

Abel whirled, frantically scanning the station for the girl, but Eris had disappeared.

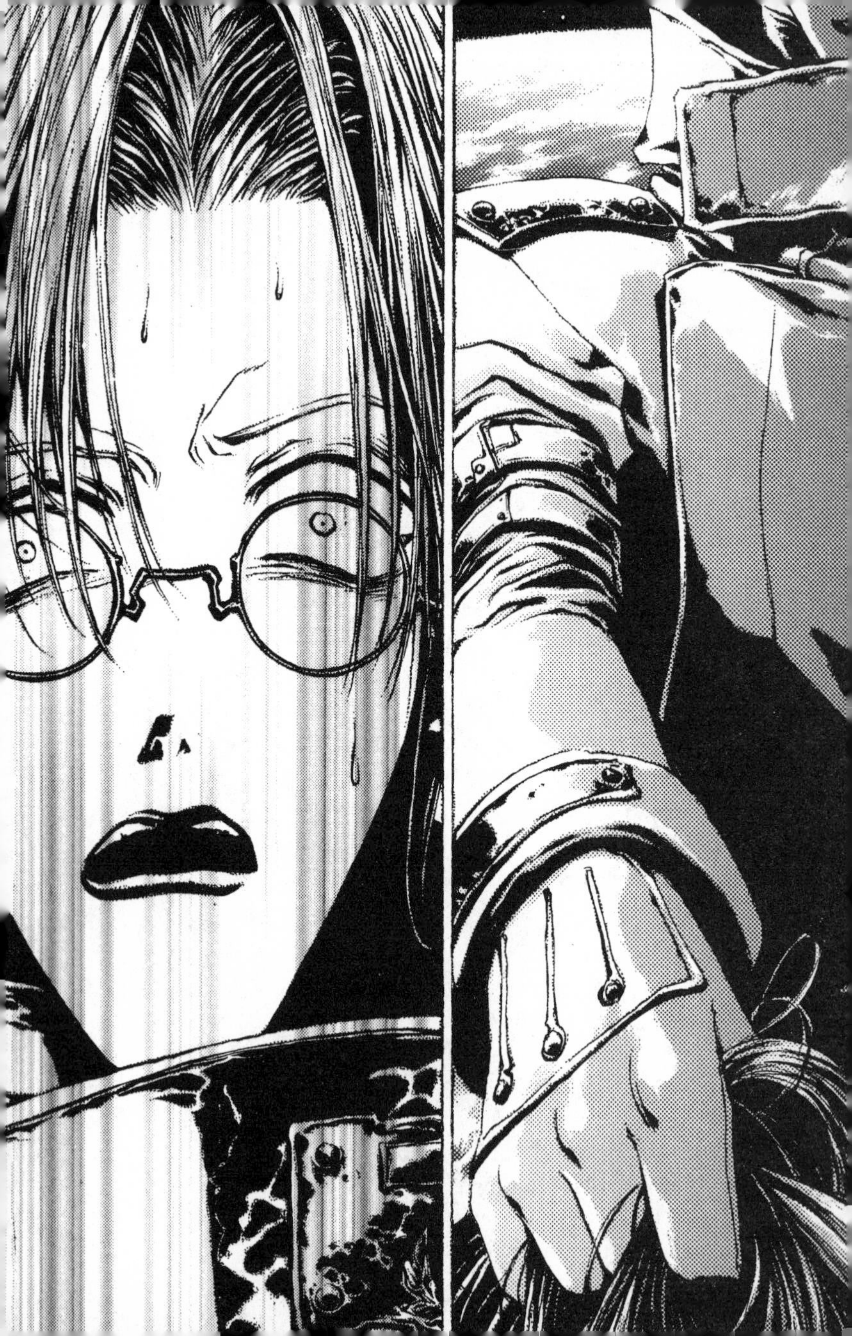

IV

I can do this," she reassured herself.

The underground passage's lights flickered. Eris kept up her brisk pace. During the day, construction workers were there, but after dark, it was empty. For Eris' purposes, it was the best route to get out of the train station.

"I can do this," she said again. She was used to running away. The bunker, a lavish house, a back alley . . . she'd had many temporary residences.

She was always alone. Occasionally, someone would care for her genuinely—until she showed her powers. Then, they'd leave her behind. Some people would even try to kill her.

"You've got me," the priest had told her. He'd said it sincerely, but he didn't know about her powers. He'd turn on her as soon as he found out, just like all the others. He couldn't be trusted.

She heard the jingling of the keychain on her bag. The little black cat snapped off and fell to the ground. It looked up at her, its eyes reflecting the flickering fluorescent lamps. Eris stared at it, unable to work up regret or remorse.

"Cheap piece of junk," she said to convince herself. *It really is a worthless piece of plastic. But it's the thought that counted, right?*

"Hmph!" she grunted.

Eris bent down to pick up the worthless plastic trinket. As soon as she touched it . . .

BOOM!

Her hair whipped around her face from the force of the bullet that had almost hit her. Eris didn't even have time to question what was happening.

A series of bluish-white flashes sparked behind her—bullets ricocheted off the walls. Eris saw a red laser cut a path to its target. She pressed her back flat against the wall.

BOOM!

She screamed as the rounds went by. Bullets struck the overhead lights, plunging her into near darkness. Eris looked down to see the red light beam rest on her shoulder. This shot would be the end of her for sure.

"Eris!" someone screamed.

A blurred figure grabbed her by the arm and spun her violently.

BOOM!

She heard the blast as she tumbled down, but she didn't land on the ground. She landed on top of a man. He scooped her up and rolled them to the cover of one of the tunnel's support columns.

She screamed again.

"It's okay. I've got you," the voice said calmly. The man scooted them both into sitting position and rested his cheek against hers. "It's okay, so please calm down," he whispered.

"Father?" She knew that voice, and the clean smell of his subtle cologne. The gangly, goofy priest was now acting like a sleek, sexy shark. It was a horribly tense situation, but he didn't even break a sweat. Eris was impressed.

"How did you find me?" she asked.

"Talk later. Run now!" Abel yelled.

Multiple gunshots rained down relentlessly. The powerful rounds turned the concrete wall into Swiss cheese.

They ran toward the next column, but they didn't make it. Abel tripped on a pipe. He collapsed on top of Eris; their legs tangled together. The sudden stop saved their lives. Beside them, the wall was riddled with bullets at chest height. Had he not been so clumsy, they would have been shredded.

"Father!"

Now in the pitch-blackness, Eris thought the priest was dead. She worried he would suffocate her with his weight. Her heartbeat drummed in her ears. Convinced she'd be shot dead because the priest's body was trapping her, she panicked.

She heard footsteps in the darkness.

An emergency lamp suddenly flickered on and bathed the area in an eerie red light.

Eris looked up to see a man pointing a gun at her face. The barrel was huge—she could easily make out the spiral grooves inside. *This is how I'm going to die . . .*

"What are you doing . . . ?" Abel asked, sitting up and clutching his thigh. A bullet had gone clean through the meat of his leg, and dark blood seeped out of the wound. ". . . Tres?"

V

Tres, what are you doing?" Abel implored.

"I checked up on the girl," Tres responded. The priest's monotone was not comforting. The smell of spent gunpowder was even more disconcerting. But what really had Abel worried was the gun pointed at his chest—or rather, pointed at Eris' head as she cowered behind him.

"The first case was two years ago. Her biological father shot her mother and killed himself: a murder-suicide. After that, she was placed in foster care. The second case was her foster father. He shot himself in the head with a hunting rifle. The third case was at her replacement orphanage. One year ago, eight boys in the orphanage slashed each other to death with kitchen knives. It was deemed a gang-related fracas, but the motives were very unclear," Tres explained.

The girl went pale as Tres pitilessly spoke about her past. She crouched behind Abel's back, unable to hold back her sobs.

"And last week's case at the safe house. Now we finally know why the vampires killed each other. It was not a territorial skirmish. This girl *manipulated* them to kill each other. Department of Inquisition has ruled that she is a witch. She is wanted, dead or alive," Tres continued.

"Your kiss? You used contact telepathy. That's how you bewitched me," Abel murmured to Eris.

Before the Armageddon, scientists were able to decipher human DNA, and they developed techniques to alter the genetic codes. "Witches" were descendents of those genetically altered humans. They developed amazing mental powers: telepathy, ESP, telekinesis, and pyrokinesis. They could, reportedly, read people's minds or move objects without touching them.

After the Armageddon, vampires and humans went to war. Both sides detested witches and hunted them ruthlessly. Global genocide resulted, leaving barely any witches alive. In rare cases, some powers lay dormant during the Inquisition; these traits skipped a few generations, and then appeared randomly in some descendents.

Eris was one such witch.

"Listen to reason, Tres! It's true—she has an unexplained power. But how can we say that *she* was responsible for all those deaths without digging a little deeper?" Abel asked.

"Intent and responsibility are not of our concern. She was involved, and she is dangerous. That is all the evidence we need. This is not our decision, Father Nightroad; this is our superiors' order. It is highly probable that the vampires at the safe house wanted to usurp her powers. She is a living weapon and cannot fall into their hands. She must be terminated," Tres said coldly.

Abel mulled Tres' words over while Eris tugged on the back of his robe, silently asking for his protection. *What if her powers can influence a large city or a Vatican military base? Is protecting one life worth that risk?*

"This girl is not human," Tres said. "She is a bomb in a human body. She is a threat. We need to neutralize her now."

Abel looked down at the ground. Tres was right, and he knew it.

"Step aside, Father Nightroad," Tres commanded.

"No," Abel replied, his gaze still downcast. He pulled his revolver from his hip holster and stood defiantly before Tres. "I promised to help her. And I keep my promises."

"Are you going fight me, Crusnik?" Tres asked.

Abel said nothing, nodding his head ever so slightly. Blown out cable boxes popped and hissed, but otherwise, it was silent.

Gunslinger nodded as well. "Affirmative. If you say so, then so shall it be."

"I didn't *say* anything," Abel argued, trying to buy some time.

"You leave me with no choice. Removing AX Agent Abel Nightroad from the friendly identification list," Tres announced.

If Tres were human, he would have shown a change in demeanor or expression. But Tres wasn't human. In a fraction of a second, his spinal CPU altered his combat program's genocide mode, though nothing outwardly indicated this.

"You have disobeyed the papal duty regulations, Canon Article 188. Abel Nightroad, you must be eliminated," Tres said.

"Tres, wait!" Abel tried to interject, but it was too late.

He hoisted Eris up and kicked Tres in the chest in one fluid motion. Abel grimaced in pain, the bullet wound in his leg burning as he exerted himself.

The maneuver didn't do much to Tres—it bought them a second or two at best.

Abel leveled the pistol, but before he could pull the trigger . . .

BOOM!

A flash of light in the darkness blinded him temporarily. His revolver was knocked so forcefully from his hands that Abel was just grateful he'd managed to keep all his fingers.

In the next instant, Abel took another blow, this time to the forehead. It spun him around.

"It is no use, Nightroad. You cannot escape me—not with your specs," Tres informed him from somewhere in the darkness. Precisely tracing Abel as he limped along, Tres fired again, and the column separating him from his targets was reduced to powder.

Abel made a move for his discarded pistol.

"You're zero point three seconds too late," Tres said.

BOOM!

"Father!" Eris screamed.

Abel lost all feeling in his left shoulder. He crashed to the floor. His arm was barely attached, but he could still twitch his fingers.

His revolver was just outside his reach. Still, he tried . . .

Then Abel felt something pop and spark on his right arm. He knew instantly what it was.

Methodical footsteps approached, then stopped two yards away. "Stand down and show some dignity, Father Nightroad."

"I've got plenty of fight left in me," Abel snarked. He wrapped his right hand around a rubber cord.

The red beam of Tres' laser sights bore down on the back of Abel's head.

Suddenly, Eris slid across the floor. She scooped up Abel's pistol and dove behind a column. It took Tres, one of the Killing Doll series, less than a second to adjust his aim on her, but it was all the time Abel needed.

A bluish-white spark viciously struck Tres in the chest.

"Zzzzzzz!"

Tres screamed, staggered clumsily, and went down on one knee. A web of sparks covered his chest and spread out like a net.

"Eris, run!" Abel screamed.

Tres writhed and wriggled like a hooked fish. Abel couldn't stomach much more; he yanked the live wire off of his former friend. He looked back, surprised to find Eris beside him.

"What are you doing, Eris?! I told you to run!"

"I'm not leaving without you, Father!" she sobbed.

He shook his head and put his arm around her shoulders.

They stumbled up the stairs and into the lobby. Just as they did, the departure bell rang throughout the station. The train blew steam, preparing to leave the platform. Both of them dripping blood, they zigged and zagged their way to Sister Louise.

"Father Nightroad, what happened?" Sister Louise asked, her mouth agape.

"Sister Louise, please take the girl," Abel implored.

"Father!" Eris protested.

Abel pushed her into the open arms of the nun, and then he turned around. He could hear Gunslinger's labored, mechanical steps.

Eris gasped. "He's not dead!" she whispered.

"Eris, *please* go," Abel rasped. He was barely able to stand, but he pushed away her outreached hands. "Please . . . run away. I'll slow him down."

He coughed. A trickle of blood dripped down his chin. *"Now!"*

Sister Louise understood his urgency, and she pulled Eris toward the train. The girls' eyes welled up with unshed tears. She couldn't thank him enough.

The priest smiled softly at her.

"Why?" she asked.

"Why what?" he whispered.

"Why are you being so nice to a monster like me?"

"You are not a monster; you're just different." Abel winked.

"Come, Eris," Sister Louise demanded. "We need to listen to Father Nightroad."

"B-but . . ." Eris stammered.

". . . Please go," Abel whispered.

She yanked free from the nun, and kissed him before he could pull away.

Abel braced himself for the worst, expecting her to use contact telepathy again., but nothing happened.

He gently nudged her toward an empty passenger car, and Sister Louise ushered Eris onto the train. He stood there and watched her lips move as the train began to pull away. Her goodbye made him smile.

The train exited the station, Eris now on her way to safety.

Abel turned around to find himself face to face with Gunslinger. He wasn't surprised, just fatigued. "It's too late—she's already gone."

"I suppose so," Tres agreed. The Killing Doll put his gun against Abel's bleeding forehead. Travelers on the platform saw this and called for security. In a matter of seconds, train station employees and security guards rushed to the scene.

"It is not over yet, Father Nightroad. I have not given up," Tres said, turning to the station employees. He lowered his gun. "Contact the next station and have them stop that train," he commanded.

"The next station? That train isn't going to another station," one employee said.

Abel's eyebrows shot up in shock. "Say what?"

"That train is out of service; it's going straight to the repair warehouse," the man explained.

"Wh-what do you mean it's out of service?" Abel asked breathlessly.

Before the train station employee could answer, a nun approached. "Excuse me; I hope I'm not interrupting something, but are you two from the Vatican Papal Affairs Department?"

Abel's jaw dropped. He already knew what she was going to say next.

"I'm sorry for being late. I'm Sister Louise from the Saint Rochelle Convent. I'm here to pick up the girl, Eris? Where is she?" the nun asked innocently.

VI

Those Vatican stiffs are such idiots," said the vampire as she tugged at her nun costume.

Mileil Manson snickered to herself. Her smile exposed the tips of her long fangs. Her laughter was not malicious—she looked more cynically amused than anything. But her jovial mood quickly turned sour.

"It's nice to finally meet you, you little monster," Mileil growled.

"No need for pleasantries, *old lady,*" Eris replied venomously. Despite being chained and shackled, she was still full of spirit. "I'll make sure to say goodbye nicely when they kill you."

"Stop dreaming." She got right in Eris' face. "We won't make the same mistakes twice. We know that you can't use your powers unless you touch your enemy," the vampire said.

Mileil grabbed the back of Eris' hair and tugged violently, until the girl was on her tiptoes. Eris yelped as the chains bit into her. Mileil, enjoying her pain, brushed her fangs over the hollow of Eris' exposed neck. "I'd love to rip your little throat out, but the Rosenkreuz Orden has other plans for you. You're going to be our ticket to leave Fleur du Mal as of today."

"Rosen-whatzit?" Eris asked, as bratty as ever. It was false bravado; she was seriously worried about just how many vampires were after her.

"There's someone who really wants to see you. Told us about your little stay in the orphanage, too," Mileil went on.

Eris started to worry. Tres was right. The vampires were going to use her as a weapon.

"Murderer! *You* killed everyone in the orphanage. I heard them talking about it," Eris accused.

"What right do you have to call *me* a murderer, you little killer?" the vampire asked. Her smile said it all. She knew. She knew about Eris' parents, her foster father, and the little boys at the orphanage. "There are piles of dead bodies in your wake. Compared to that, vampires are practically saints." Mileil laughed.

Eris wanted to snap back, but she just bit her lip. Maybe she deserved to be called a monster. All those deaths *were* her fault. Her ability to get into people's hearts and twist their emotions caused all of those tragedies.

In fact, her parents weren't even the first victims. There had been a priest in the village who had molested her. He killed himself horribly, stabbing a knife through his heart. After that, her parents made a suicide pact in order to escape responsibility for their daughter's freakish powers. Neither one wanted a witch for a daughter. Her foster father's suicide was self-defense. When he'd discovered she was a witch, he tried to kill her with a hunting rifle. She'd used her powers to make him take his own life. Finally, there was the incident at the vampire safe-house. She'd never forget that pungent, rotting smell.

"You have no one to turn to," the vampire whispered into her ear. "You're a monster. You're neither human, nor a vampire. You're alone."

Eris looked around nervously.

The landscape was dark, bleak. Eris saw several other vampires milling about the train. She had counted at least ten. Even if she used her powers on Mileil and escaped her bonds, she couldn't possibly make it out alive.

"I *am* alone," she whispered. Her eyes brimmed with hot tears. She'd gone through so much, just to get killed this way.

She didn't want to die alone.

"Eris!" someone yelled.

She knew who it was instantly.

"Who the hell is that?!" Mileil screamed.

Abel held on tightly to the wing of an aircraft, his long hair and priest's robe whipping in the wind.

"Vatican!" screamed the vampire.

The *Iron Maiden* pulled alongside the train. The sleek airship could easily have blown the train from its tracks, but Abel had a different plan. He clutched at one of the lower wings, hovering just outside the train's window.

"Sister Kate, move us in closer!" Abel yelled over the whipping wind. "I'm going to jump! Get us as close as possible!"

"I can't get you any closer, Abel! Besides, I still haven't gotten confirmation that this mission is sanctioned. You cleared this with Cardinal Caterina, right?" Sister Kate asked.

"It's approved!" he lied. "I'll get her authorization later," he muttered under his breath.

"What did you just say?" Sister Kate asked.

But Abel had already leapt, crashed through the window, and toppled inside the train. His landing was far from graceful. Abel's body careened through the seats, severing them from their metal foundations. He stopped smack-dab on his face. Without a word, he stood, cracked his neck, and raised an eyebrow.

Even the vampires were impressed.

"Father!" Eris shouted gleefully.

The vampires surrounded Abel. They hissed and spat at him.

"Why did you come, Father?" Eris asked breathlessly.

He smiled at the girl. "I told you, you've got me. Isn't that reason enough?"

He had an air of strength about him, despite the pathetic bandages that had been hastily wrapped around his shoulder and leg. Fresh blood seeped through the dressings. It was clear that he was far from one hundred percent, but he acted like he could fight the very devil himself.

"Either you're brave or just plain stupid," Mileil said. She screeched loud enough to rattle a man's teeth. Instantly, her fingernails grew, stretching as long as knives. She stabbed her twelve-inch nails into the wall, twisting and rending the sheet metal like it was paper.

"You'll die alone, Vatican. And so will this witch!" Mileil cackled.

Abel didn't so much as blink. "You must be members of Fleur du Mal, right? You're under arrest for eighty counts of murder, blood extortion, and kidnapping. I strongly recommend that you drop your weapons and turn yourselves in at once," he said calmly, fixing his glasses and adjusting his sleeves.

"Eleven against one? I don't like your odds, Vatican." Mileil smiled.

"Whoever said I was alone?" Abel asked.

BOOM! BOOM! BOOM!

Huge, unerring bullets whizzed though the compartment. Vampires were cut in half, sometimes two at a time, by the raw force of firepower.

The roof crumbled in on itself. Tres fell into the compartment, a pistol in each hand. He adjusted his aim and fired without pause.

BOOM! BOOM! BOOM!
BOOM! BOOM! BOOM!

Bits of vampires splattered all over the car. The blasts were deafening and blinding. Nothing could survive such a merciless barrage.

Tres divided his lines of fire, launching bullets in two directions at once.

"Don't kill them all, Tres!" Abel shouted above the din.

"Affirmative. I have many questions for them to answer," Tres responded. He paused to reload.

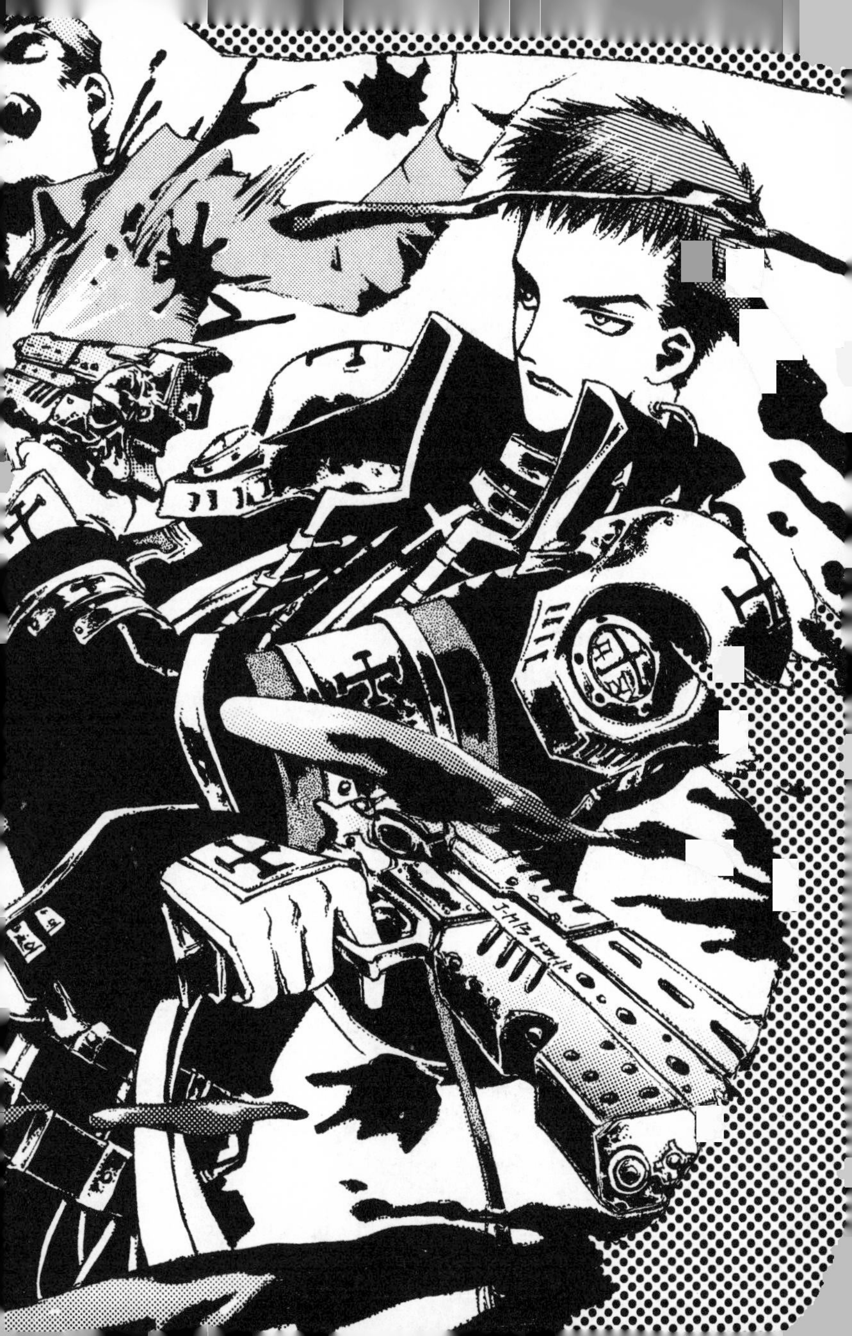

Every single vampire writhed in pain, but they were all still alive. Some even had enough energy to fight back. Seizing the opportunity, a vampire came out of hiding and pounced on Tres' back.

"Too late," Gunslinger said. With a flick his wrist, his gun's magazine dropped from the grip's cavity. The next moment, a fresh magazine popped out of his spring-loaded sleeve and snapped into the gun. Aiming at the ceiling directly above him, Tres squeezed off three rounds. The roof came tumbling down, pinning the vampire to the floor.

"Grah!" the creature screamed in dismay.

After that, Tres leveled the remaining vampires. It only took another ten seconds and ten bullets. When he was done, the only people left standing in the train car were Tres, Abel, and Eris.

The glass-eyed Gunslinger surveyed his handy work. "Clear. Switching from genocide mode to search and destroy. Status report, Father Nightroad?" Tres asked coldly.

"Not a scratch from the firefight. Are you okay, Eris?" Abel looked the girl over for any injuries.

"Look out!" Eris screamed.

Mileil sprung up from the blood and guts on the floor. "Go to hell!" she screamed. Swiping with her claws, she lopped the head off the pinned vampire, then brought her other hand around and to split a hydraulic line on Tres' shoulder.

His gun dropped to the floor.

Abel's jaw dropped in disbelief.

Sparks burst from Tres' torso as she scraped his chest plate. Eris tried to intervene, but a stray fingernail sliced her shoulder open. Eris screamed and dropped to her knees.

Tres tumbled and tried to point his pistol, but Mileil kicked it out of his grasp. "Too slow!" She brought both sets of claws high into the air and prepared to stab Tres and Eris both.

Then her chest exploded.

Mileil's eyes widened as her heart ripped in half.

"Tres, please take the girl outside," Abel said calmly.

The priest—tall and thin, with long hair and round glasses and a normally soft gaze—now wore an expression as hard as stone. His fist protruded from the vampire's chest cavity. Ribs and guts hung limply from his forearm. He was buried up to his elbow in the vampire.

Mileil tried to speak, but her lungs had burst open. She was silently dying, her eyes rolling, searching for her killer.

Abel glanced at Eris with cold blue eyes. "Gunslinger, please *take the girl outside,*" he said again.

"Father Nightroad? You're not going to . . . ?" Tres asked with an unusual hint of surprise.

Eris wouldn't budge. She crossed her arms defiantly. "I want to see it," she insisted.

"I am quite sure you don't, Eris," Tres said.

"It's okay, Tres. Let her stay," Abel relented. He looked deeply into Eris' eyes and then began his ritual. "If I get out of control, please . . ." Abel said to Tres.

"Affirmative," Tres answered.

"Father?" Eris asked, suddenly frightened.

"Eris, I need to show you something." Abel extended his fingers and slowly removed his arm from the half-dead vampire's chest. "You and I are alike. I am also haunted by powers within me—cursed powers that try to devour my soul from the inside out," he explained.

His eyes changed color, fading from winter blue to blood red.

"But I have not given up on living. I can't hide from my sins. If I give in, I'll be nothing more than a monster. But I choose to live as a man. I *choose* to live with the burden," he whispered.

Taking a deep breath, he murmured, "Nanomachine Crusnik 02 forty percent limited performance—authorized."

A dry cracking noise filled the blood-soaked railcar.

"My God," Eris whispered.

"No, not God," Abel replied.

Mileil, free from Crusnik's fist, tried to stagger away, but fell limply to the floor instead.

Abel kneeled over her, his hand inches from the ground. The vampire's blood sprayed—undulating, coiling, twisting—drawn to pool in the center of the rail car. Abel's palm acted like a magnet, attracting the dark liquid. He lowered his palm into the puddle and it began to suck up the blood.

"Ever thought about it? Humans eat animals. Vampires eat humans. What if there was something that ate vampires?" Abel asked aloud. "Something higher up the food chain?"

The floor was spotless now, not a drop of blood to be seen.

Abel rose slowly. "I am a Crusnik—a vampire that feeds on other vampires."

"No way!" Eris exclaimed.

Mileil had healed enough to try to escape. She didn't get far.

With a sound like bending metal, the priest's right arm split open up to his shoulder. He didn't bleed; instead, the opening glowed darkly. From a pocket dimension, a double-bladed scythe sprung up into the priest's hand. There, the blade waited for its master.

"You reap what you sow, Mileil," Abel said.

He brought the scythe down in one fluid motion, so flawless and graceful that it seemed to defy physics.

✝

"Are you okay, Eris?" Abel asked. The bloodstained priest reached out to the girl. As he did, his eyes returned to their winter-blue color. "Your shoulder was injured. We need to take care of that," he observed.

"Did you kill her?" Eris asked.

"No, actually. I just incapacitated her," Abel said proudly.

"*Who* are you?" she asked, stepping backward.

In that moment, Abel Nightroad's heart broke. Not because Eris stepped away from him, but because of the nature of her question.

"What are you?" Eris clarified.

"I'm a human being," he whispered, reaching his hand out farther, a brittle smile stretching his gaunt face. "Just like you."

Eris ran to him. He enveloped her in a hug, and they looked for all the world like a long-lost brother and sister finally reunited. "Don't get too close. You'll get dirty. I'm filthy," he warned.

"You're perfect," she sobbed, nuzzling him. "If you're dirty, I don't want to be clean."

Abel stroked her hair and took a deep breath.

Unfortunately, the click of a pistol's hammer ruined the touching moment.

"Tres? Are you still convinced she's dangerous?" Abel asked, threading his fingers through Eris' soft hair.

"Affirmative. I told you—her intentions do not concern me."

Abel turned to look at Tres. His laser pointed straight between Eris' eyes.

"We must eliminate dangerous elements as much as possible," Tres said. The Killing Doll emotionlessly pulled the trigger.

Abel tried to push Eris away, but he wasn't fast enough.

CLICK!

Nothing happened.

Abel blinked at Tres. They exchanged a long look.

"Out of ammo. The elimination cannot be accomplished at this time," Tres concluded.

Abel sighed, relaxing his shoulders. He knew better than to think that Gunslinger had actually run out of ammunition. "Thank you, Father Tres."

"Negative. It won't happen again," Tres said. The android stared at Eris for a moment, warning her silently, then walked away.

"Raaaaaaah!" Mileil roared. She leapt up, her broken claws extended. It was an impressive display of fortitude and hatred, even for a vampire. But it didn't last long.

"Eris!" Abel screamed.

Tres moved like lightning. He didn't waste time turning around. A spring-loaded clip launched into the air from his wrist driver. As it did, he brought his M13 around in midair. The clip sprang into the empty cavity and a round chambered instantly. Tres fired a shot within the blink of an eye.

BOOM!

He fired another, then another. Each M13 shell struck the vampire's body, batting Mileil's frame around like a shuttlecock. Bullets pierced her brain and heart, finally killing her.

"Mission complete. *Iron Maiden* is waiting," Tres said over his shoulder.

Abel and Eris shared a frightened glance, both thinking the same thing: *Good thing Gunslinger is on my side.*

FROM THE EMPIRE

. . . all the earth shall perish, for a deluge shall come upon the whole earth, and all things which are in it shall be destroyed.
—Book of Enoch 10:2

The streets of Venice were packed with masked revelers that night. Firecrackers and sparklers bright enough to outshine the two moons illuminated the basilica and palace.

"Barbaric Terran," Asthe spat out.

Festive sounds wafted along the breeze, carried into the alley where she waited.

Vampire travelogues gave Asthe a general idea of what the Venetian Carnival was, but upon actually seeing it, she thought it was a ridiculous event. Asthe couldn't understand the Terran; she didn't understand the appeal of drinking all day and night for ten straight days.

"The meeting had to be here—of all places—and the contact is late," she muttered.

In Asthe's homeland, daily business started when the sun set. Here, however, the day began with the dawn. In the distance, she could hear the sound of bells ringing out, signifying midnight. It was a beginning of a new day for the Terran.

Her contact was very late. Irritated, she raised her leather coat's collar and removed her sunglasses. She did her best to blend in.

Her contact was supposedly one of *them*.

Is he really an AX agent? Even with all the legends surrounding the elite group, Asthe was convinced he would be a weakly Terran, hardly worthy of note. She could probably do this job alone, but it was in her best interests to work with the Terran, so she waited.

If he's not here in five minutes . . .

It had taken centuries to find religious fanatics who would listen to their side. Many people would be upset if she went back empty-handed.

"The sooner I leave this monkey mountain the better." She nodded to herself.

Asthe's ears perked up upon hearing voices in the dark canal. Two women were arguing with four gondoliers. After taking a few seconds to decipher their slang, it sounded to Asthe like the women didn't have enough money for the fare and were being asked to pay the difference with sexual favors.

Asthe didn't care about the problems of a few Terran street whores. But it did bother her that they were close. She thought seriously about killing the lot of them just to shut them up.

Then Asthe heard another voice join the conversation. "Um, excuse me. Can you give me some directions? I'm looking for the road to the Saint Mark Plaza?" It was a tall young man with thick glasses and a poor priest's robe. He was a little young to be a traveling priest. "Venice is such a maze. Are you going to the festival, too?"

"Hey, Father, we're a little busy here," said a bearded oarsman. "Ask for directions from someone else, all right?"

"Well, but . . ." the priest stalled.

"Oh, Father! Please help us!" one of the girls yelled. Both women ran toward the priest. They pleaded with tearful eyes and clung to his worn-out robe. "Please help us! They want us to—" the other girl started.

"We want them to pay for their ride. Anything else they say is a lie!" one of the oarsmen shouted.

"Hm . . . Why don't you cut them a break, just this once?" Abel offered.

The oarsmen, riled up by liquor and the thought of sex, were not easily swayed. They stepped forward. Abel held up his hands in a gesture of peace. The girls grabbed each other and shook from fear.

"Violence isn't the answer, guys. Please turn the other cheek," Abel reasoned.

The oar swung around quickly, but Abel ducked it easily.

"Run, ladies," he commanded.

"Don't you go anywhere," the bearded oarsman said menacingly.

But now it was too late for the gondoliers. The ladies' colorful dresses fluttered in the wind as they rounded a corner and disappeared into the plaza.

"Problem solved," Abel said. "The ladies are gone. You guys have nothing to be mad about anymore. Let's just all go home."

The oarsmen slowly surrounded Abel like a pack of wild dogs.

"Guys, guys, guys. Let's talk this out," Abel said.

"Get him!" the bearded oarsman said.

"It's a sin to fight a priest," Abel whispered as they closed in.

Oars thumped into flesh with a sickening *smack*.

Poor bastard. Asthe couldn't curb her curiosity any longer. Besides, she didn't want all that blood to go to waste. She looked around for other passersby, but it was safe. *My contact is late, so I might as well have some fun.*

Asthe ran silently, her legs inhumanly powerful. She was at least ten times as strong and agile as a Terran. Asthe kicked off the alley walls, picking up altitude, her body soaring through the air. She landed on the thugs.

The bearded gondolier was the first to notice, but it didn't do him much good.

She backhanded him before he could say anything to the others. Asthe intended the blow to be a light one. She just wanted to knock him down, but she must have misjudged her own strength, because his orbital bone shattered and his left eye popped out. He was probably dead, but she just shrugged. *Oh well.*

She paused and looked at the other drunken ruffians. They clearly couldn't believe their eyes.

Asthe was dazzlingly beautiful and she knew it. At least six feet tall, with a long black coat that hung down to her heels, she was an alabaster goddess. Her hair was ivory colored, except for a stripe of red that hung down over her face. She looked young, barely out of her teens.

"Who are you?" one of the gondoliers finally mustered the courage to inquire.

"Step aside," she commanded.

The oarsmen were too stunned to move.

"Too stupid to know when to run," Asthe muttered to herself.

Within a few seconds, the oarsmen were unconscious.

"Stupid Terran."

She'd seen it on their faces just before she beat them senseless. They knew what she was. The word on the tips of their tongues was *vampire*. Such an ugly word. *How dare they slur at a mighty Methuselah?*

She licked a drop of blood from her knuckles and groaned in pleasure. Diablerie was the perfect form of eating. It was an art. *How dare they profane the majestic Methuselah with their animal grotesqueness?*

"Um, excuse me," Abel said from the ground.

Asthe barely turned to regard the pathetic priest.

"If you don't mind, could you help me up?" he asked.

She didn't want to get involved in Terran matters; she rolled her eyes at her own stupidity. She should have let the gondoliers kill the priest and rape those foolish whores.

Silently, Asthe reached her hand down. "Here, hang on," she said.

"Thank you."

He started to continue, but she waved him off. "Be gone, and be thankful for my mercy," she said.

"Of course," he said, his expression totally deadpan. He started to leave but turned around and asked one last question.

"Are you from the Methuselah Empire? You aren't, by any chance, Astharoshe Asran, Duchess of Odessa and Kiev, undercover agent of the New Human Empire?"

Asthe's jaw dropped.

Only an AX agent could recognize her true identity in this part of the world. *How does this schmuck know?*

The realization made Asthe narrow her eyes with contempt. "Cardinal Caterina promised a skilled agent to aid in our bilateral operation," she said. "You're an idiot who can't handle four drunken rowers."

The priest smiled at her. "So it is you, Astharoshe. Wonderful. I was worried that you had already left. I am Father Abel Nightroad. Cardinal Sforza ordered me to assist Your Grace with the investigation in Venice. Pleased to meet you," Abel said.

Asthe seriously wondered if this wasn't some elaborate joke. Much to her chagrin, she soon discovered that he truly was her partner.

I

There had been a series of murders in Venice, all of which implicated a vampire as the killer. Two weeks ago, the tide gate manager at the Moses Dam, which separated the lagoon and the outer sea, went missing. His body, sans head, had been recovered—drained of blood.

The second incident was worse. The dam's entire night shift, twenty men in total, had been massacred. They were flayed from the tops of their heads to the soles of their feet. The company was rumored to have ties with organized crime, so it was initially believed to have been the result of underhanded business dealings gone badly. Some of the corpses still hadn't been identified. Autopsies concluded that exsanguination was the most common cause of death.

The third incident was the death of an assistant archeology professor at the Venetian College. He and his family were killed in their home five days ago. According to the police investigation, the assistant professor made counterfeit antiques on the side, but there were no other details.

In all three cases, the bite marks matched. It was believed that this was the work of one killer, or a group of killers working together. Vampire killings were rare, but not unheard of. One clue, however, pointed the investigation in an uncomfortable direction. The professor was wearing a ring bearing the emblem of a foreign, *non-human* country.

"So, this is it?" Asthe asked, perched on the edge of her gondola seat. She snatched the moonstone ring from Abel's open palm. It was easy for her to make out all its laser-etched intricacies. The base's design depicted two moons, one large and one small—the symbol of the New Human Empire. The top of the ring showed a dragon holding a sword and dagger. This was the symbol of Count Zagrev's family. Only nobles were allowed to have such a ring.

"This is, without a doubt, his ring. You humans don't have the technology to forge this sort of design," Asthe said. "Hey, are you okay?"

Asthe looked on with contempt as her companion threw up over the side of the gondola.

"Oh, sorry. I get sick on moving objects," Abel fibbed.

"Worthless," Asthe grumbled.

Their gondola reached a wealthy neighborhood. It was quiet, unlit; most of the residents had left for the carnival.

Venice was an ancient city, long under Vatican control. Below sea level, the city streets were filled with water and could only be navigated by small boats. Even the poorest house had a porch leading to a canal to board or disembark on watercrafts.

"This will be fine," Abel said to the gondolier. Then he turned to Asthe. "This is the site of the fourth incident."

They stood in front of a large mansion. Asthe looked up into the night sky. The moon above moved ever eastward. She didn't have much time before daybreak.

"Eight hours ago, a groundskeeper found the body. Cardinal Caterina pressured the Vatican, who in turn pressured the Venetian police. The locals have left the crime scene undisturbed for us," Abel said.

The priest fumbled with a bunch of keys, eventually opening the door. An unmistakable stench leaked out of the room.

"Marco Colleoni was Venice's top antique merchant and appraiser," Abel said.

The house brimmed with valuable antiques. The killer clearly wasn't a robber.

Seconds later, the motive became clear. On the ground next to Marco's body was a message written in blood; a large, red upside-down cross and *Igne Natura Renovatur Integra,* which meant "with our fire, we will renew the world," were scribbled on the floor.

The letters were big and bold. Colleoni's blood wasn't the only source of paint. The rest of his family, drained dry, lay beside the cross. Even the Colleoni baby.

"This is not surprising. If the count is the culprit, this is actually quite tame. It was much worse when he impaled three hundred Terran in our homeland," Asthe said dryly.

Abel could barely breathe at the sight of the murdered infant, but Asthe blankly assessed the situation.

There was the couple with their throats slashed, their son with his eyes and heart torn out and a spike rammed from his crotch up through his mouth, their younger son with his entrails strewn about, and their baby with its skull crushed.

No doubt, these were the methods of Endre, Count of Zagrev—the Empire's worst slaughterer.

Asthe knew this was potentially devastating. The Vatican would chalk this slaying up to whatever excuse she fed them, but eventually murders like this could lead to a full-scale war between the Empire and the Vatican. She had to stop Count Zagrev as quickly as possible.

"Domine me lequit kasas miseri insanctis amiqui. Amen," Abel whispered.

Twirling her bangs in frustration, she tried to dismiss her companion. "Okay, Father, thank you for guiding me here. I'll take care of the rest. You can take a break," she said.

"What?" The priest looked completely dumbfounded. "No, I'm going with you. It's easier that way."

"This is a Methuselah problem. You were only a guide. I don't want you getting mixed up in this mess," she countered.

"It's really no trouble," Abel insisted, batting his eyelashes with boyish exuberance. "It's okay to share the burden with me. After all, we're partners," he said.

"Partners?" she asked angrily. The salty taste of blood spread in Asthe's mouth. She couldn't keep her fangs retracted.

Calm down. She took a deep breath.

She knew that her companion's statement was innocent enough, but it stung. The ugly, dopey Terran couldn't possibly understand the hallowed meaning of "partner" to a member of Methuselah society. She knew she shouldn't get irritated over such a trivial faux pas; it was like getting mad at a child.

"Don't ever use that word again," she hissed.

"What word?" Abel asked honestly.

"Don't ever call me your partner, you putrid Terran!"

Abel tried to step back, but Asthe grabbed him by the collar. She forcibly drew him within an inch of her face. "You consider someone a partner only if you can trust them with your life! An imperial noble cannot have a lowly Terran like you for a partner!" she barked.

The squirming priest's face turned blue. Asthe released her grip.

"I–I'm sorry . . . I didn't mean to offend you . . ." he whispered.

A wave of self-doubt crashed over Asthe, but she refused to acknowledge it or show signs of remorse. There was no more time to waste on this Terran dog.

"Enough. Step aside and be quiet," she commanded, kneeling near the corpses.

She ignored the bloody mess and carefully scanned each body. She looked for point of injury, torn clothing, vampire bites. They were all violently damaged, but there was nothing unique about the attacks.

When she touched the baby's body, she felt something hard. There was something inside its mouth.

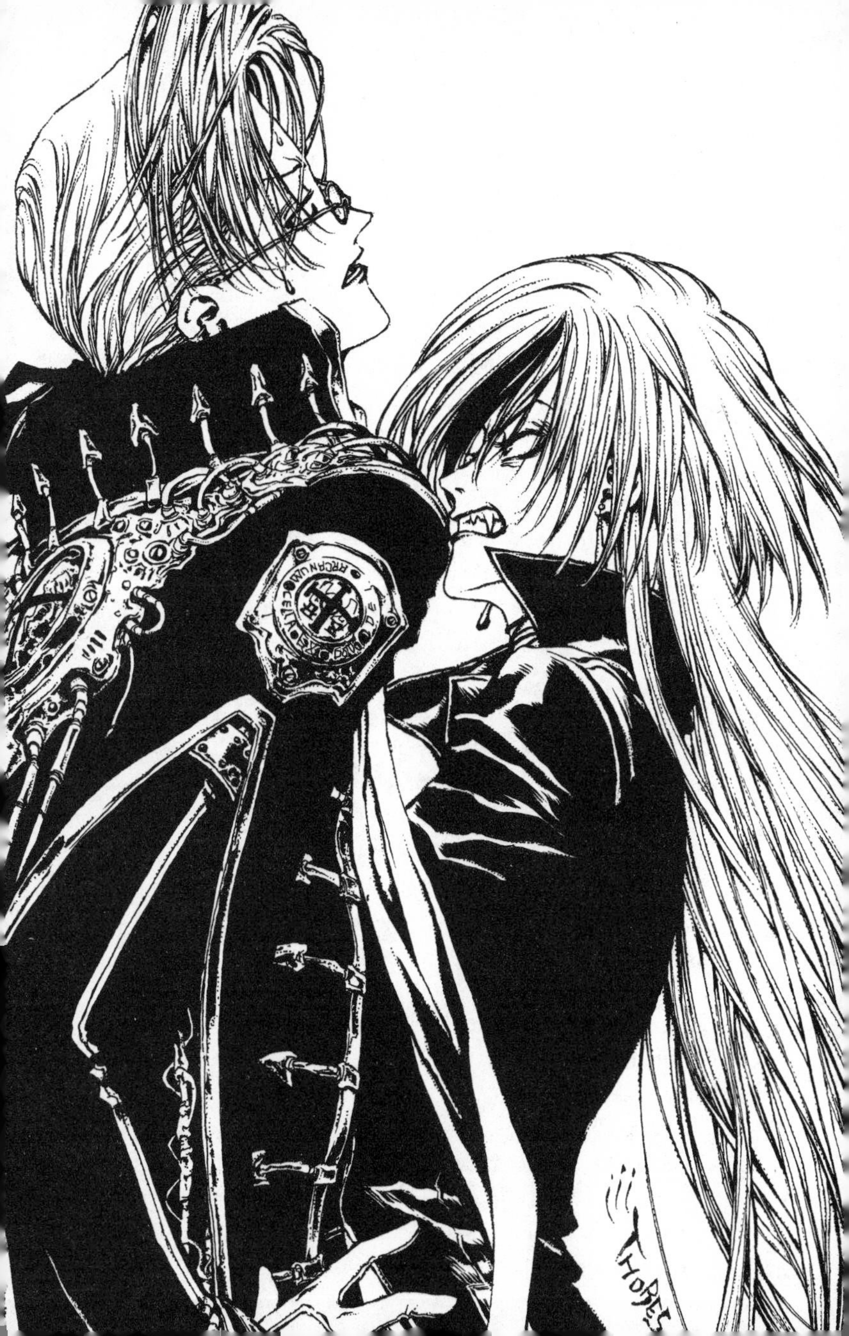
ARCANUM CELLA
THORES

"A medal? Or is it a coin?" she asked under her breath.

Asthe didn't recognize what sort of currency it was. Unlike a Vatican dinar, it was cheaply made and very light. Carved on it was an image of Jesus, crucified, and the letters *I.N.R.I* which she knew stood for *Iesus Nazarenus Rex Iudeorum* or "Jesus of Nazareth, King of the Jews."

Among the Terran in her country, it was customary to place a coin in the mouth of the deceased, so the person's soul could pay the fare to cross the river Styx. *But do these Terran also have the same custom?*

"Hey, where does this—?" she asked Abel, but stopped in mid-sentence. Her eyes locked onto the wall behind Abel. She stared at a family portrait. "Wait a minute," she said.

There in the faded silver placard sat the Colleoni family, wearing their best clothes. Marco looked like a typically stern, middle-aged father. Sitting next to him was his sympathetic daughter. In the back row was the eldest, loyal son. Next to him were his faithful wife and the newborn infant.

Then there was the younger, rebellious second son.

"Is something wrong, Asthe?"

"The corpses don't add up," she said.

"What?" Abel asked in disbelief.

"There's a body missing. You didn't see the young girl, did you?"

The teenage girl in the portrait had adorably large eyes; she looked the very picture of innocence.

"Where's the girl? Why wasn't she here?" Asthe pointed to the blood-smeared floor.

"I'll check the case notes," Abel replied. The priest flipped through the thin file for a few seconds before stopping on a page near the back. "Her name is Foscarina Colleoni. She's seventeen. She ran away from home about a month ago," he read.

"Ran away?" Asthe repeated.

"Yes. It says she had an argument with her father over her new boyfriend."

"Why would they argue over that?" Asthe asked, becoming more and more exasperated with the priest.

"Well, uh . . . you must have different views on sex and marriage in your country. It's a long explanation, but, uh, if you must know . . ." Abel trailed off, looking like a deer in headlights.

There was no point in learning Terran customs, so Asthe just shook her head. "Don't bother. Where is the girl now?" she asked.

"Unknown. The parents did some investigating, but she hasn't been found yet. 'Last seen hanging out near her boyfriend's job . . . at a casino called INRI,' " he read. The priest finally noticed that Asthe was leaving. "Wait! Where are you going?" he hollered after her.

"Back to my hotel. I've run out of time today." She frowned as she opened the front door. The sky was turning slightly blue, and farther along the canal, birds began to chirp. The cursed sun was slowly pushing away the merciful darkness.

"Tomorrow . . . I guess for you that makes it tonight—we'll go to the casino. When the sun sets, meet me at my hotel," she said as she boarded the gondola.

II

While the Saint Mark Plaza, with its palazzo and basilica, was considered the face the Venice, the canals were the heart of the city. Beneath the surface, Venice was a city of consumption and greed, and Rialto Bridge was the center of that dark underworld.

Underneath the large arching bridge that spanned the Grand Canal, several shops, clubs, restaurants, casinos and whorehouses lined up—one after another. Gaudy lights lit up the strip at night.

A tall man in a "tactician" mask gracefully disembarked from his gondola. His neatly-tailored charcoal suit and hip-length black cape contrasted sharply with his white mask.

The Tactician descended a marble staircase that led to a darkened study beneath the seedy street. There, he saw a young boy who casually had his head propped up on a rosewood desk.

He was a very handsome boy. Even in the dim light, his face seemed to glow like an angel's. He looked ten or eleven years old, but his brassy-colored eyes betrayed a thousand year's worth of evil.

"Would you like a drink?" the boy offered.

"I restrict my consumption of wine on business trips," the Tactician replied.

"That's too bad. Then again, I suppose you Terran cannot appreciate the taste of *this* delicious drink," the boy ventured, his words honeyed and his meaning full of venom.

The boy—Endre Kourza, Count of Zagrev—curled his upper lip, revealing his fangs. He lifted the decanter off the desk, poured a thick red drink, and downed it in one gulp. "Venetian. Good quality." The count laughed.

The Tactician guessed, "The appraiser's daughter?"

"She said she wanted to go back to her family. So I arranged a family reunion of sorts," the count joked.

Giggling, the count covered his mouth with his delicate hands.

The long-haired Tactician reacted indifferently. He shrugged, staying all business. "Count, will you please refrain from drawing any undue attention? Last night, a visitor from your country arrived. Do you know a young lady by the name of Astharoshe?" the Tactician asked.

"Astharoshe?" Endre raised an eyebrow. "Astharoshe Asran? Hah, they're taking me lightly, aren't they? I can't believe that they sent a young girl, just weaned on the taste of blood, to find *me*. Has my country exhausted all its good agents?"

"The problem is not Astharoshe herself. The Vatican moved to bring her here, and that's the major concern. Your Excellency, you have been making yourself known these past few weeks— quite obviously, it was your intention to lure the girl here," the Tactician continued.

Endre stuck out his tongue. *So what if he knows my exploits?*

He scratched his head and said, "Well, I've got strange ties with her, you know. I was thinking about showing her the completion of the plan."

"That's it? Your Excellency, do you know the special sub-sect of the Vatican that brought her over—AX Agency?" the Tactician asked.

The count rolled his eyes. "Never heard of it."

"The Vatican designed a special agency with the express purpose to fight us. They are the only organization that has enough power to go against our Orden. Now that they are involved, your plan may be jeopardized," the Tactician warned with great patience.

"Mister Kampfer." The count finally addressed the Tactician by name.

"Yes, Your Excellency?" Isaak Fernand von Kampfer instinctively knew he'd overstepped his bounds.

Endre didn't raise his voice even the slightest, but he had Kampfer's full attention. "Mister Kampfer, are you admonishing me?" the boy asked.

"Not at all, Your Excellency," Kampfer said.

"Then be quiet. I don't think you lowly monkeys understand the pride and honor of being a noble in our country," Endre said condescendingly. The boy sighed and sat back in his chair. "The people of my country . . . just because I killed three hundred Terran, those fools called me a monster! I must show them what justice really is! Otherwise, this plan . . . everything I've worked for . . . all of it will be in vain."

"As you wish. My sincere apologies. I forgot my place," Kampfer groveled.

"As long as you remember it now." Endre took a slug of blood right from the decanter. "I'm quite satisfied by you Orden people. I wouldn't be here had you not helped me when I was exiled. I will heed your words concerning discretion, Kampfer. Don't be upset, my friend," Endre said.

"Yes, sir." Kampfer bowed.

"*Igne Natura Renovatur Integra.* The Empire and the Vatican are both in my hands. They will shed blood and make war with spikes and swords. From the blood and fire, I will establish a new order. A power that the Empire and the Vatican couldn't even amass!" the boy yelled.

He was starting to get drunk off the smell of blood and his own scheming. Dark thoughts clouded his eyes.

The Tactician recognized this. He wisely bowed and left.

✝

"We wear masks on top of masks," he murmured, then chuckled.

The Tactician passed a couple holding hands as they stepped off their gondola. One wore a glamorously adorned "sweetheart" mask and the other sported a beak-like "doctor" mask.

He giggled. "We have to hide our identities in order to touch the world. We're so adorable, aren't we?"

"I don't care what you spout, sir, but please don't include me in your abject 'we,' Doctor," she hissed.

The Sweetheart stepped onto the street, and swatted the Doctor's hand away. "Stop touching me! Filthy monkey!" she growled.

"It's a couple's party, dear," the Doctor reminded her. The Doctor rubbed his stinging hand, his blue eyes wincing underneath his mask.

"Welcome to club INRI," the doorman greeted. "You must be new customers . . . Do you have an invitation?"

The Doctor presented an envelope.

The doorman took it and raked the Doctor with his gaze. He could tell the man was a fop at best—the sort who tried too hard to impress people, stumbled over his long clothes, and inhaled hors d'oeuvres at parties. Clearly, he was unused to wealth.

But, the Sweetheart he escorted was a creature unlike any other. Even for the doorman, who was used to noble ladies and gorgeous escorts, she was a sight to behold.

Her long, ivory hair was swept up and adorned with a glamorous string of jewels. Several finely crafted bracelets dangled on her thin wrists. She wore a diamond tiara and a dangerously low-cut, red Venetian evening dress. She was aggressive yet elegant: a walking gem.

The doorman allowed them in.

Abel stumbled past him, while Asthe glided by.

But once they passed earshot, the vampire beauty began spouting profanities. "My damn feet hurt! How do human women wear shoes like this? This place stinks like an ass! Are they smoking cigarettes? Are all Terran just plain stupid? Don't they know what it does to your lungs?!"

Asthe's voluptuous lips spouted one vulgar comment after another. She didn't pay any attention to the neo-classic furnishings or the ladies and gentlemen laughing at the roulette and baccarat tables.

"Asthe, you don't seem to be in a good mood," Abel deadpanned.

Her glare could have wilted a flower. "Whose fault do you think that is?"

She had wanted to break in undetected, but her partner insisted on making a grand entrance from the front door. She reluctantly agreed, but that was before she'd learned that rich Venetians dressed up in such ridiculous clown suits.

"Dammit, this is embarrassing," she grumbled. "If you mess this up, I'll have your head!"

"You're just a ray of sunshine, aren't you?" Abel grinned.

"That's a serious insult where I come from, Nightroad. Anyway, where is this guy? Let's get this over with," she said.

"His name is Georgioni Russo. He's a roulette dealer," Abel murmured.

The man in the golden "Casanova" mask was standing in the center of the hall, just to the side of the roulette wheel. Asthe nodded and stomped forward, but Abel frantically grabbed her arm and held her back.

"Wait, where do you think you're going?!" he whispered.

"I'll grab him by the throat and shake the info out of him. Don't worry, I'll drag him someplace quiet to interrogate him," she said dryly.

"It doesn't work like that in this country! Please let me handle this," he said, but she wasn't paying any attention. She was fixed on the Casanova.

Abel snapped his fingers at Asthe. "Hey, I have a favor to ask," he said.

She sighed, distracted. "What is it this time?"

"If we find the target, please don't arrest him today," he said.

"What?!" she screamed loudly enough for other people to shoot them a curious glance. Several security guards looked them over.

Asthe, not believing the priest's outrageous request, barely restrained her urge to rip off his head. She opened up her fan and brought her pearly red lips close to the ears of the Doctor. Resisting the temptation to bite his ear off, she whispered, "You saw the same murders I saw! There will be more victims if we don't catch him now!" She looked around to make sure no one was staring at them anymore. "This is the last Carnival day. It's too dangerous to let him get away tonight. If the Methuselah got mixed up into this mess, what do you think will happen?"

One Methuselah equaled the strength of an entire Terran military unit. If a band of Methuselah went all-out in this fiasco, it would result in nothing short of urban warfare.

"Once we find out where he hides, we can call for reinforcements. So it's better for us to just run surveillance tonight . . . please?" Abel begged.

She did not reply.

"Asthe?"

She pouted as she scanned the room full of grinning masks. Eventually, she turned back to face the priest. "I suppose tonight we'll just find him," she said through gritted teeth.

"Excellent. Shall we?" he offered his arm.

She ignored it and walked toward the roulette wheel.

"Excuse me, Mister Russo? Can we talk for a second?" Abel asked politely.

Russo spun around and lost his breath when he saw Asthe. He gulped audibly and bowed deeply. "What can I do for you?"

Asthe elbowed Abel in the ribs—hard—and stepped forward.

"You're too gullible, Doctor." She focused intently on Russo. "Where is the girl called Foscarina? I heard that you two were lovers. I want the truth."

"Are you the police?" he asked.

"No, we're—"

"—friends of the family!" Abel interrupted. "And, from a small town, too . . . yes. Um, and she is Foscarina's older sister. She was kind of concerned about her sister's disappearance."

"Foscarina's sister? Wait . . . she had a sister?" Russo asked incredulously.

"Yes. We came down from the mountains the other day, wanting to visit for a while. So, would you know where we might find Foscarina?" Abel asked.

"I told the police everything," Russo said plainly. "Foscarina wasn't my girlfriend. She was the kind of girl I'd call when I was drunk, y'know? She was really into me, but that wasn't my fault. You have sex with a girl a few times, and she thinks she's your girlfriend. What a pain. Excuse me; I need to go back to work," Russo said smugly.

"Hey, hold it right there." Asthe reached out to stop Russo. She didn't care about the love affairs of Terran, but the way he talked irked her. She wanted to grab the Casanova by the collar and beat some manners into him.

But Asthe's fingers never touched him. Instead, a fist popped Russo in the nose and sent him sprawling to the floor.

Asthe was shocked. "Father?"

Abel looked down at his clenched fist, bewildered. "Did I just do that?" he asked innocently.

"You bastard!" Russo yelled.

Security guards grabbed Abel. One of them locked Abel's arm behind his back. Another kicked him in the stomach.

"Gwarg!"

The groan didn't come from the priest. The guard that had kicked Abel got poked in the throat with a long, elegant finger. He covered his neck in agony.

Asthe smiled. "I like this."

Security guards swarmed the casino.

Asthe's dress was perfect for fighting. The high seams in her skirt kept her legs unrestricted enough to kick a man in the face. So she did. Repeatedly.

"Why, you—uck!" A guard stopped short as her heel met his nose.

"You insolent wretch!" she screamed.

One guard grabbed her, only to go airborne in the next second. The gossiping wives in the casino's bar shrieked in horror.

WHOOOMPH!

Asthe hurled another across the room. She ducked a heavy left hook and responded with an uppercut to the guard's jaw and a knee to his gut.

A dozen more guards appeared. Asthe, undeterred, waded into the fray. "Peons! So many peons!" She grunted, punching the first one in striking distance.

She saw Russo running to the far end of the hall. Her fangs gleamed. She had a problem with killing a dozen or so Terran just to wrap up her investigation. That said, she didn't want to go easy on the guards or let the target get away. She had to find a happy, non-lethal medium. *What a bother.*

"Go get him, Nightroad!" she yelled.

"What?" Abel shook his head as he took out another guard.

Asthe grabbed the priest's robe, shaking him like a doll before tossing him across the room. Abel felt like a hurtled discus as he landed heavily on a poker table. Chips and cards bounced up in the air. The grizzled gamblers stood and rolled up their sleeves. They didn't speak. They didn't shriek in protest. They just wanted to beat the living crap out of this priest for disturbing their game.

The remaining security guards tackled Abel. They tried to restrain him and the angry poker players at the same time. It was chaos.

"Please calm down! Everyone, please calm down!" Abel yelled in vain.

Amid the confusion of the casino, Russo escaped.

✝

Russo huffed and puffed as he ran. "Dammit. Who the hell was that woman?!"

There was nobody else in the fourth floor's darkened corridor. It was the owner's personal floor. Russo was one of the few staff members even allowed up there.

After double-checking that no one was around, Russo knocked on the oak door. "Excuse me, boss. It's Russo. I need to tell you something."

"Enter," the boss said.

The door creaked open.

"What's going on downstairs, Russo?" the boss asked.

The room was pitch-black, just like always. The boss didn't seem to need any lights on.

"There was a lady asking after that girl," Russo said.

"A lady? Was it a young woman with white hair?" the boss asked.

"Yeah. Do you know her?" Russo asked.

"I think so. Was she wearing a red dress and a sweetheart mask?" the boss asked.

Russo gasped. "Y-yes! How did you know?"

"Because she's right behind you, you idiot!" the boss screamed.

"Wha—?" Russo couldn't turn around. His boss' small hand had reached up and crushed his throat.

"I'm so sick of Terran stupidity. Anyway, long time no see, Astharoshe," Endre said.

"Count Endre, I finally found you," she said humbly. Asthe pulled out a silver rod that she had concealed on her upper thigh until this very moment. "You know what this is, Endre. You should come quietly," she snarled.

He grinned. "The Sword of Gae Bolg, eh? Our misguided countrymen let you bring over such a weapon? Did they really think that a cheap little whore like you could handle me?" Despite his bravado, Endre was impressed.

Asthe's rod began to glow bright red. Slowly and seamlessly, it transformed into a sword. "Die!" she screamed.

Then the office exploded.

III

At first, everyone outside the casino thought it was a Carnival firecracker. By the time they realized it wasn't, the windows of the magnificent mansion were reduced to scattered shards.

People along the walkways and in gondolas below looked up and began to chatter among themselves. But, thanks to the explosion, no one noticed two shadows jump into the darkness.

Asthe leapt like a lioness and ran along the sidewalls of the mansion's exterior, her movements too fast for the human eye.

Vampires could "hasten" their bodies for short periods of time. They stimulated their body's nervous system until it kicked into overdrive. By doing so, they increased their speed tenfold. For example, back in the office, Asthe had swung her sword down fast enough to break the sound barrier.

Her weapon, the Sword of Gae Bolg, had been a Kiev family heirloom. The sword was a plasma jet system with xenon gas ionized by a laser that streamed out from a vacuum core. The high-temperature–high-density plasma could slice through anything; it was the ultimate weapon. Out of the relics found from the Empire's lost technology, this was the strongest close-combat weapon recovered.

And now, the ionized xenon gas coming out of the sword's tip trailed a large red whip through the air. The plasma licked at the ancient childlike vampire, as if driven by Asthe's will.

Endre went into haste mode and left the room before the sword shattered his desk and all the glass on the floor. Even with his lead, Asthe kept close behind. He could hear the jet stream of xenon gas burning through the cold night air. She would catch him if he didn't do something drastic.

He jumped from a great height and made for a nearby canal, timing it perfectly to land on a gondola. Then he leapt away again. Unfortunately for the passengers, the gondola split in half and sank.

"You're not getting away that easily!" Asthe yelled.

She dove toward the canal, shooting a jet of plasma from the sword as she did. The water's surface vaporized under the extreme heat. Amid the instantly formed fog, Asthe kicked off the river bottom and jumped onto a nearby bridge.

"Damn you! Where are you?!" she bellowed.

Coming out of haste mode, it must have seemed to the Terran that Asthe had appeared from out of nowhere. Revelers stopped and stared.

Her dress had been torn to shreds during the intense explosion. What was left of her mask clung to her face, barely holding back her disheveled hair. Asthe wasn't concerned about her appearance, however.

She tried to catch her breath.

Dammit! Where is he?

She had only been in haste mode for about a minute, but she had used up too much energy. All the synapses in her nervous system were burning. Still, she had enough pain, hatred, and anger to continue on.

"I'm gonna kill him. I swear it. He's done for!" she yelled defiantly.

Oddly, she hadn't intended to harm Endre until she'd seen him a minute ago. Even then, she'd actually suppressed her urge to kill him. She wanted to arrest him and take him back to the Empire. That was her mission as an undercover agent.

But once she saw his face and heard his voice, something burst inside her.

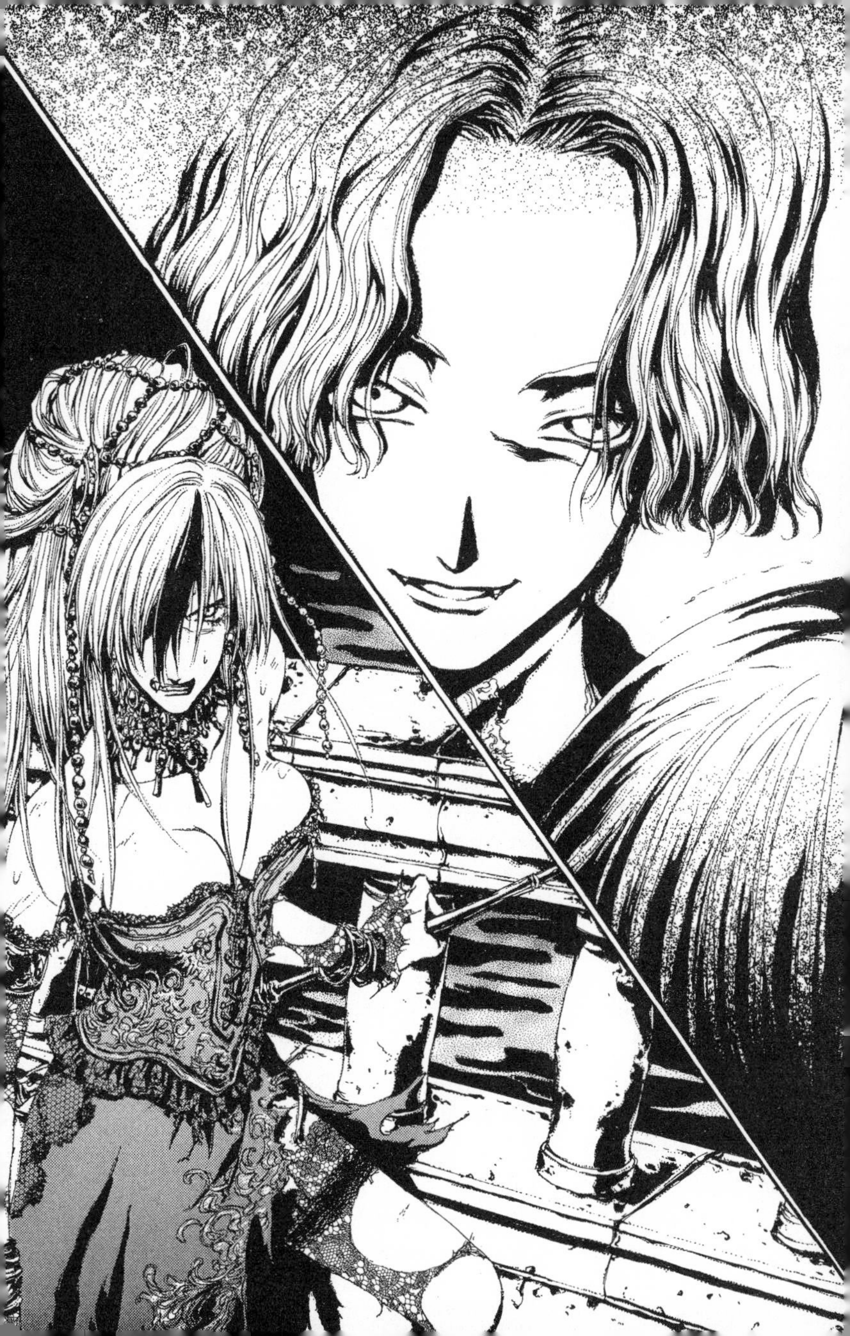

Where did he go? She'd been right behind him.

"Are you looking for someone?" Endre asked.

Asthe was startled to see an evil shadow perched atop the stone bridge's high arch. To most people, he looked like a cherub. They would have been fooled by his innocent face, but his brass-colored eyes belied pure evil.

"Oh, this is so nostalgic. It was a pretty night like this last time," he said smugly.

Asthe glared at the boy. His mention of the past stung her.

Suddenly, Endre revealed a captive—a young girl, less than nine or ten years old. She had simply been in the wrong place at the wrong time. Endre removed the terrified girl's Carnival mask and licked the tears off her face.

"What's wrong, Asthe? You're so calm all of a sudden. Weren't you going to kill me a moment ago?" He grinned.

Asthe clenched her jaw. *Déjà vu.*

"Back then, Astharoshe, you were trembling in my arms, and young Countess Len Yearnosh was in your position now. She was your partner for how long?" he prodded.

"Stop it," Asthe commanded.

"Isn't that what the countess said? She was quite protective of you." The ancient vampire snickered. "And I told the countess to lay down her weapon if she wanted to save your life, and she did."

"Stop!" she repeated.

"I don't think so," he replied.

Endre's claws tore into the girl's cheek. A red trickle ran down her white skin. Astharoshe had bled the same way.

"Then I split her head open, remember?" the count asked.

"No!" Asthe yelled.

Up on the vault, a red geyser spurted, and the young girl's head popped off.

Asthe didn't waste any time. She swung the sword and unleashed a blast of plasma. The vault of the bridge blew away. By then, though, the boyish vampire was gone.

"Damn it!" Asthe yelled.

She started to give chase when she heard Abel yelling, "Asthe! Don't go after him! He'll only kill more innocents! Did you forget your promise?"

"Promise?" she choked out. "I lied." She jumped into haste mode and chased after the small shadow. Her long strides quickly made up the distance.

"Endre!" she screamed, trying to break his concentration. "I'm coming for you!"

Asthe blasted the walls that held the canals in place. Liquefied stone and debris plunged into the water as she continued to chase Count Endre. She ignored everything but the small shadow that ran from her.

"You'll pay for that girl's life—for all the girls' lives!" she threatened.

It seemed like they ran for an eternity. Her body and brain screamed in agony, but finally Endre's speed slowed; he was reaching the limit of his haste mode. Ironically, they had returned to the bridge that she'd just blasted. Many Terran milled about, but despite that, Asthe swung her sword without hesitation, heedless of casualties.

Endre, once again, disappeared.

The ionized xenon whip cracked in the night sky and the smell of burnt oxygen hung thickly in the air.

Where did he go? She looked around frantically.

"It's over, Astharoshe," Endre said.

Asthe turned to glimpse her own shadow in the river; next to her, she saw a smaller shadow.

He was above her.

She had no time to look up; she just instinctively flicked the sword. The ionized xenon gas found its target. A gigawatt of electricity would burn the elderly vampire to a crisp.

But instead, he laughed.

"Too slow, Astharoshe Asran," Endre mocked.

She saw that her plasma blast had been fractured and bounced in streaks upon Rialto Bridge, rifling past the several hundred people who were crossing it.

"Aegis shield," she spat out.

Eight silver orbs surrounded the boy-vampire.

He had an Aegis shield—soft, glowing orbs that orbited Endre like planets in the solar system. The orbs' magnetic shield had dissipated the powerful energy of the sword.

One of the rebounding sparks came directly for Asthe. She silently apologized to her dead partner and promised to meet her in the afterlife. Before she was struck, Asthe fell out of haste mode and lost consciousness.

As she passed out, she heard the priest call her name.

IV

Asthe?"

Asthe wondered why her dead partner was calling her. It didn't make sense.

"Huh?" she groaned.

The blackness turned to a light blur; the blur eventually became clear. Her face was covered by some kind of cloth. Then she caught his scent. "Father Nightroad?"

"So, you're awake," he responded. His glasses were broken, but his eyes peered at her softly, without blame. He smiled weakly.

Where are we? It looked like a combat zone—nothing but debris and blood.

"Endre! Where is he? Oh . . ." she moaned.

"Don't move," he quietly bade her. He held Asthe's arm still when she tried to get up. She felt a sharp pain in her stomach. Then she registered the bandages that were wrapped around her waist. She winced. One of the orbs' reflections had probably hit her. It left a horrible burn.

"I applied some first aid," Abel said. "A Methuselah will recover from this, but please stay still until help arrives."

"Stupid! We have to go after Endre now . . ." she objected. She felt so woozy; it stood to reason that she'd lost a lot of blood in addition to getting burned. Still, she had no time to let the priest play doctor. *Endre must be stopped!*

"Out of the way, Father! I must . . ."

His unusually strong hand held Asthe down. His voice, in contrast, was gentle. "Asthe, have you not killed enough already?"

"What?" she whispered. Eventually, she understood what he'd meant. Thin metal supports poked out from the rubble, eerie voices screamed, water rushed through the streets—this part of Venice looked like a bomb had gone off.

In actuality, the Sword of Gae Bolg had gone off.

The last remnants of Rialto Bridge crumbled into the canal. The stores lining the bridge had been completely destroyed and collapsed into the water while she'd been unconscious. But the real horror was *between* the rubble.

There were hands sticking out, begging for help. A young couple embraced each other as they were crushed to death. Mothers held their babies as they blistered and burned to ashes. People cried out, looking for lost loved ones or missing limbs.

"Father? What happened?" she asked. Asthe looked down at her bloody hands. *Did I do this?* "F-Father, did I . . . ?" She couldn't say the words. Her eyes welled up with tears.

No answer came. The priest simply closed his eyes.

" . . . Father?" she begged.

Asthe noticed fresh blood was seeping into her pores and healing her wounds. *Whose blood is it?* Surely a Methuselah like herself would thirst and lose control after such an ordeal.

It was Abel's blood.

"F-Father!" She jerked in shock.

Abel's body slid off her. She saw the Sword of Gae Bolg piercing his torso from behind . . .

She blacked out again.

✝

"This is Your Eminence's itinerary for the visit to Venice two days from now. The visit to the tide gate is at the same time as the big Mass, but if you wish to see it during high tide, this is the only available time," the secretary said.

"It's fine. I don't mind," Cardinal Caterina Sforza said. She crossed her legs and smiled reassuringly to her secretary.

"If I attend the Mass, the duke of Florence will probably go nuts. Let's let the bishop of Venice take care of the ritual," she reasoned.

The secretary chuckled softly. Caterina and the duke of Florence, her half brother, Cardinal Francesco di Medici, were known for their squabbles. In particular, they fought about their younger brother, the current pope.

"Excuse me, Your Eminence. This came from Venice." A squire brought forth a note.

Usually, this time of day was scheduled for her to meditate, but as the Vatican's Minister of Foreign Affairs, Caterina had an endless line of visitors requesting an audience. She glanced down at the memo and nodded.

"Is that it for reports?" she asked. "Good, then. Everyone, carry on."

Once the staff finished their morning reports, they left the church. Alone, Caterina stayed behind for her meditation. Instead, she lightly pressed her finger against her temple and spoke.

"Sister Kate?"

"Yes, Your Eminence," came the disembodied response. It was a hologram of Sister Kate standing before the altar. She smiled at the cardinal. "Regarding Father Nightroad . . . did he accomplish his mission so quickly?"

"Bad news . . . There was an incident in Venice," the cardinal replied.

"I'm bringing up a visual now . . . Holy God! Did a war break out?" Sister Kate asked.

"I don't know. But the Empire had something to do with it, for certain," Caterina stated.

The New Human Empire—the largest territory that vampires controlled—was the only non-human nation on the plant. With an abundance of vampires who possessed technologically advanced weaponry, the Empire was quite dangerous.

To the Vatican, the paragon of humanity, the Empire was a threatening enemy. Both nations were embroiled in a centuries-long Cold War. They had not clashed head-on, but it was sure to happen someday. The Vatican's mission was to prepare for such a conflict.

Cardinal Caterina boldly moved to create a mutually beneficial diplomatic pipeline with the rival nation. If found out by her peers, it would mean death by firing squad for her. Especially if Francesco ever found out. He would gladly oust his sister and dissolve AX Agency at the first opportunity.

A papal trial was surely in her future if anything went wrong with this tenuous alliance.

Even so, Cardinal Caterina hazarded the risk because she knew of a third, more deadly enemy. Once the world learned of it, humans and vampires alike would tremble in its wake.

Her current plan had to be carefully crafted and guarded with the strictest secrecy. She informed the Empire of a criminal hiding out in Vatican territory, and asked to have one of their undercover agents arrest him.

Even for such a simple operation, sacrifices had to be made.

It was all over now. There had been open fighting during Carnival. It had been a colossal failure. *Is it my fault? Am I to blame for trusting a vampire to value human lives?*

Regardless, even Caterina's political influence couldn't cover up such a fiasco. She would have to destroy the evidence before Department of Inquisition started digging.

"Sister Kate, hurry to Venice. Secure the imperial agent," Caterina said.

"Understood. Count of Zagrev is still at large. Will the vampire agent be willing to return empty-handed?" Sister Kate asked.

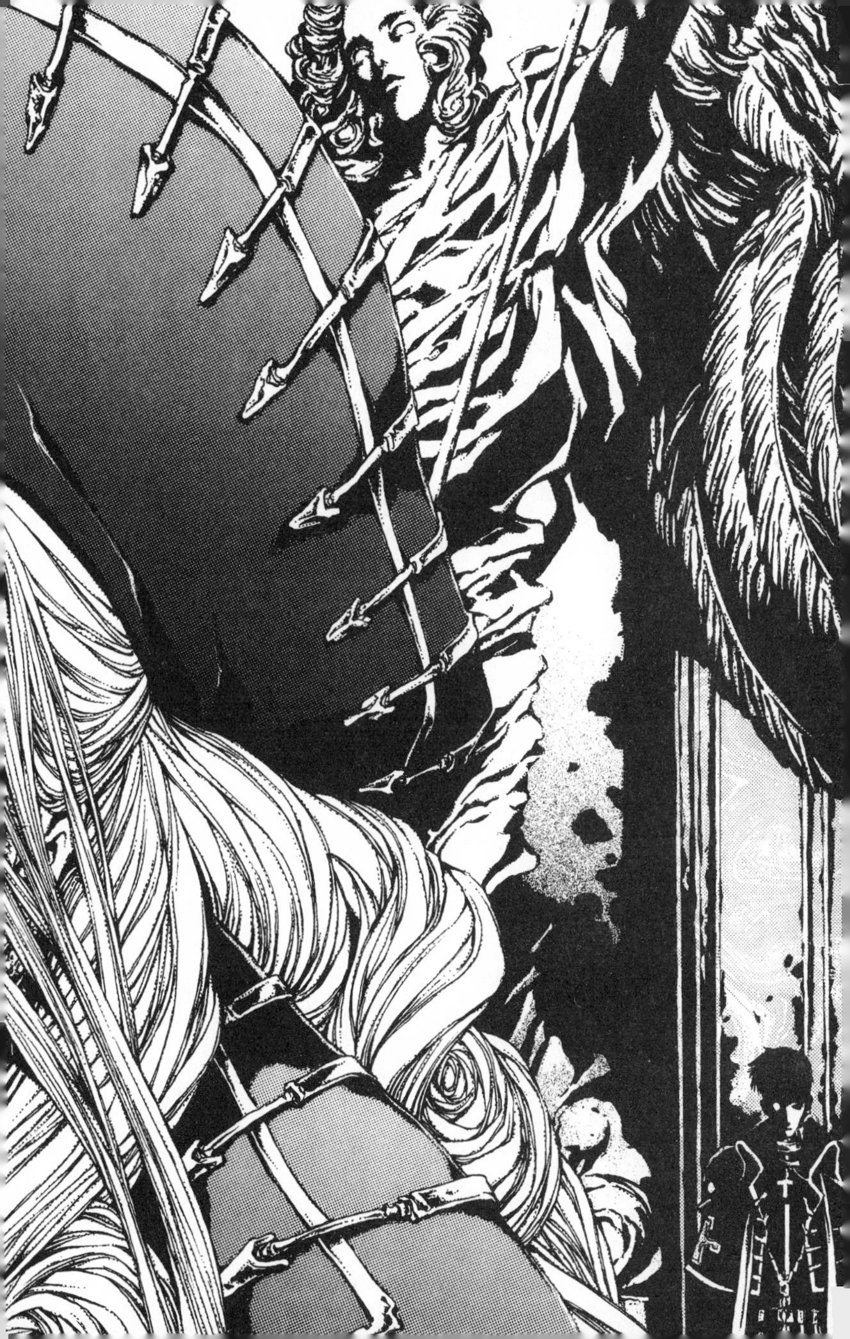

"She doesn't have a choice in the matter. Secure her and escort her to the imperial border. If she refuses to return to her homeland . . ." She let the sentence hang in the air for a moment. Then she faced Tres, also known as Gunslinger or the mechanical Killing Doll, who sat motionlessly in her office. "You know what you need to do,"

"Affirmative," Tres replied. His voice was dry and emotionless. As always.

V

Sometimes the month following Carnival would be chilly, but this year, spring came early. Weather like this caused an *acqua alta*. During high tides, the sea waters overflowed the canals and drenched the city streets.

"This must be it," Asthe said.

She splashed through deep puddles as she scanned for the number to the correct ward. After rounding a few corners, she walked up to the front desk, not even bothering to remove her sunglasses even though it was nighttime. "I would like to visit a patient," she said.

"What is the patient's name?" the nurse asked.

"Abel. Father Abel Nightroad." Her voice cracked as she spoke.

The hospital was empty at this time of night, except for the most dedicated family and friends. Asthe's footsteps echoed in the silent hallways.

She came to a tiny, bleak room and paused. She could hear faint voices inside.

" . . . dead . . ." one said.

"Trying . . . save the girl . . ." another said.

Without knocking, Asthe opened the door. "Abel?" she whispered.

Mourners stood around the bed. They turned to regard Asthe.

"Miss, do you know our son?" an elderly woman asked.

Asthe saw the dead body of a young man, but thankfully it wasn't the priest. Tears stung her eyes. Asthe recalled the deceased young man's face, and the young girl sobbing at his side . . . The young man had tried to save his girlfriend during her fight with Endre last night.

"I-I'm sorry. Wrong room," she stammered.

"Will you stay and pray with us?" the old woman asked.

"Oh, I . . ." She fumbled for the words.

What should I say? He's dead and it's my fault.

Perhaps oddly, most vampires valued life as much as humans did. They were not killers by nature; they just hunted food to survive. And with their incredibly long lifespans, a funeral was a morose affair, packed with hundreds of mourners who had come to know the deceased over many decades. Any Methuselah's death was a great tragedy.

"Um . . . I'm sorry," she said finally.

"It's okay. Anyone can wander into the wrong room," the old woman consoled. "There is another young man in the room next door," she offered.

"O-okay. Thank you. Pardon me." Asthe excused herself and left quickly. Her legs felt like jelly as she walked to the adjacent room.

"Hey there, Asthe," she heard.

She peeked into the open room and saw that a familiar smile awaited her.

"I'm so glad to see you. Did you come here for me?" asked Abel.

"You seem chipper," she said honestly.

"Thanks. It only hurts if I move." He laughed. "The doctor says the piece of glass that scratched me was inches from my heart. I'm lucky to be alive."

"I see . . . That's good." Asthe paused.

He'd lost a lot of blood for just a simple scratch, but she didn't question him since he was alive and well.

"What's wrong?" Abel asked.

"Well, you know, the Terran . . ." That was the wrong way to start the conversation, so Asthe began again. "So, Terran also mourn death?" she asked.

"Yes. We're very similar in that respect. We laugh when we are happy. We cry when we are sad. And sometimes, we act out of revenge. We are no different," Abel said.

She decided to leave the rest unsaid. Instead, she murmured, "I can't find Endre."

"Unfortunate," was his only reply.

It had been over twenty hours since they'd fought. She couldn't find him, but what chance did she have? She had no connections in this world. The count had been networking for some time.

It all seemed very funny to her now. Asthe had always looked down upon the Outers—humans that weren't part of the Empire—but she didn't know a thing about them. Propaganda comprised so much of their education that they weren't much use in the real world. Even if she could speak their language, she couldn't talk about the simplest things.

"I'm such a fool," she whispered.

The priest had been so good to her, but she'd mocked him. He'd helped an outsider get settled in comfortably, kept in touch with his agency, and set things up so that they almost caught Endre. It was *her* fault that she'd ignored his advice and caused such tragedy.

"I'm such a fool!" she said more forcefully.

"Pardon?" he asked.

"Nothing," she replied, wiping away a tear. She forced a smile and shook her head.

She couldn't bring up the real reason for her visit now. The body in the other room was evidence that she didn't have the right. Thinking this would be her final conversation with Abel, she said what she truly felt. "Father, I mocked you." She bit her lip, resisting the urge to ask for his help again after she'd put him in a hospital bed.

"I'm really sorry. Thank you for everything," she said finally. Asthe bowed and turned to leave.

Who knows how long it will take to find Endre? She would probably be killed if she did catch up with him on her own, but Augusta's orders were absolute. It was her honor and duty to carry out this mission. She was at rest with her cruel fate.

"Wait, Asthe," Abel pleaded.

Asthe looked back hesitantly. "Wh-what are you doing?"

Abel was removing his pajamas. "I'm trying to change clothes. Turn around; it's embarrassing to have you stare at me."

"Idiot! You're in no condition to move yet!" she scolded.

"You don't want to see your partner in pajamas, do you?" he asked.

"Of course not! But . . . ?" Asthe trailed off. "Partner?" she asked. "You're still willing to help me?"

"Of course I am," he said resolutely.

Asthe didn't know how to respond.

Abel gave her a thumbs-up, then rubbed the back of his neck, chagrined. "Sorry. Guess I wasn't supposed to say 'partner,' huh?"

Asthe was taken aback by this Terran. She wanted to hug him, but she didn't know how that vampire custom would go over in the Vatican's world. So she stuck out her hand and offered it to Abel.

"Thank you . . . partner," she offered.

He placed his hand in hers and shook it with a rather firm grip for a man at death's door. "You're welcome . . ." They stared into one another's eyes for a moment, then awkwardly dropped their hands. "Where will Endre go?" Abel asked.

"He'll definitely head for Rome," she replied.

"We should check the airports and train stations. But why Rome? Any reason?" Abel asked.

Just then, the door swung open. Asthe instinctively shielded Abel and drew her sword. The smell of gunpowder filled the small hospital room.

"Tres!" Abel yelled at the figure in the hallway.

Tres entered the room, gun drawn.

"Asthe, this is Tres, er . . . Gunslinger. Luck is on our side! If he's with us, then we're practically invincible. Tres, this is Asthe, she's from . . ." Abel was cut short.

"She is Astharoshe Asran, Duchess of Odessa, undercover agent for the New Human Empire—I'm aware," Tres said coldly. The android never wasted any time with redundant greetings. "Situation update, as of now: Vatican AX Agency has ceased support for the duchess of Odessa . . . cooperation is over. Duchess, you are to return to your homeland immediately," Tres recited.

✝

" 'Sleep under the lagoon, Venice. The sea god brings darkness in the flow of night. The breaking waves sing eternal death.' Maurice Barres," Kampfer quoted. His recall of poetry was unmatched.

The misty sea breeze lifted his long black hair. Thin, drifting clouds covered the two moons.

"It will be quite windy come midnight. We are fortunate," Kampfer said. He turned to his companion and grinned. "You will arrive safely, Your Excellency."

"Even if I succeed, the whole plan will fail if you fail, Kampfer," Endre warned. His voice sounded like that of a choir boy's, but his rancid smell contrasted sharply with his youthful beauty. The thick scent of blood mixed with the salty air. In the darkness, sharp fangs reflected pale moonlight.

"What do you think of my disguise?" Endre asked.

"It looks wonderful, Count. Nobody will suspect. Shall we go? It's about to rain," Kampfer suggested.

"I hate saying goodbye to Venice, Kampfer. It really is a wonderful town," Endre opined.

"You must say goodbye in more ways than one." Kampfer winked, tossing his cigar overboard. It trailed a line of smoke before splashing into the sea. A wave rolled over it, extinguishing the red-hot ash.

Asthe dropped a pill into her glass of mineral water. It bubbled and danced before turning the fizzing water a deep ruby red. She took a few sips, then tilted the glass back and downed the whole thing. Methuselah Life Water always tasted bitter to Asthe.

She couldn't sit still. From the window, she could see a lit airstrip that stretched out to the sea. Despite the late hour, a plane was landing. A long line of people waited at the waterbus stop en route to Venice.

Carnival was over, but lots of folks were still out.

"I'm sorry, Asthe," Abel offered.

"It's my own fault. There was nothing you could do," she replied. She put her remaining blood capsules back into her pill case and tried to force a smile.

She'd failed, and she could only blame herself. She would have to pay for her foolishness and arrogance. It was inevitable.

"This is the *Iron Maiden*. Father Abel, refueling is almost complete," Sister Kate said into Abel's earpiece.

Asthe could easily hear her soft voice.

"We will probably depart in about ten minutes. Please board soon," Sister Kate instructed.

"Understood, Sister Kate. Where is Tres?" Abel asked.

"He went to the control tower to delete the flight records. I'd like the two of you to board first."

"Shall we go?" Abel motioned for Asthe to go on ahead of him.

The airport was busy. A sinking feeling welled up in Asthe as they walked through the terminal. "I trust you to resolve the Endre case, Abel," she said.

The lights from Venice flickered atop the surface of the ocean. It was quite peaceful, even charming.

Unmoved, Asthe silently seethed. "Use any means necessary," she whispered. "Kill him if you have to. Don't hesitate. Too much is at stake."

"I will do what I can," he answered honestly.

There wasn't much to go on. They'd gotten nothing from the casino crime scene. They learned nothing from the fiasco at the bridge. The count's whereabouts were still unknown. They couldn't even tell if he was still in Venice.

"He will definitely go to Rome. You can't let him enter Rome," she said.

They walked through the bustling crowd.

"You said as much back at the hospital. What's in Rome? Rome is the Vatican's stronghold. The security is too heavy for him to try anyth—ah, I'm sorry!" Abel apologized. The priest bowed apologetically to the nun he'd bumped into.

Asthe shook her head at her goofy partner. "Why is it so crowded? Is it always like this?" she asked.

"No, tonight is special. There will be a large Mass at the Saint Mark chapel," Abel responded.

"Large Mass? Two nights ago was Carnival, and tonight a large Mass? Terran are always celebrating something." She chuckled.

"The holy remains of Saint Mark were missing for years, but they were rediscovered last month in Rome. Tonight is a celebratory Mass for their return," Abel explained. "Saint Mark was one of the twelve disciples of Jesus, one of the writers of the Bible, and was the Patron Saint of Venice. His remains were stored in Saint Mark Plaza's bascilica, and many people believe he protected this town by making several miracles happen."

They passed another aircraft full of pilgrims. "These travelers are flocking here to see the revered Saint Mark," he concluded.

"But it's only old bones, right? Why are you guys honoring a set of bones that you're not even sure are his? You Terran never cease to amaze me." She chortled.

"How rude! You shouldn't make fun of our rituals like that. Scientists have repeatedly analyzed the bones to ensure authenticity, and the remains are officially being escorted back to their proper burial place by His Holiness," he said.

Asthe stopped walking and grabbed Abel's arm. "What?" she asked.

Abel looked at her like she was crazy.

"What did you just say?" she asked again.

"Well, uh, tonight, there will be a large Mass to return the body—" Abel started.

"After that! You said, 'escorted by His Holiness,' right? Do you mean the pope?" she demanded

"Yes. His Holiness arrived in town from Rome, and will personally conduct the Mass to safely return the body. It was in all the newspapers," he said.

She rushed to a newspaper vendor. Sure enough, the front page of that day's paper showed a pimple-faced boy sporting a weak smile. It was Pope Alessandro XVIII.

"Holy crap," Asthe swore. She didn't realize that her fangs stuck out. *"This* is what he was waiting for," she growled at Abel.

"Who's waiting?" Abel asked stupidly.

She grabbed Abel's shoulders and pulled him close. "When is the Mass? When is the pope going to conduct it?"

"Just after midnight."

She turned on her heel and dragged him forcefully behind her. "We have no time. The pope is in danger," she said as they ran.

"What are you talking about?"

"Endre committed genocide against the Terran, that's what he's notorious for, yes. But he was exiled from the Empire because he was guilty of *treason*. Don't you see?" she whispered, exasperated. She'd been ordered to never reveal the real reason for Endre's exile, but she was past that now. "He was secretly trying to start a war between the Empire and the Vatican. That's why Augusta banished him."

"What does that have to do with the Saint Mark Mass?" Abel asked.

"Stupid, don't you see?!" Asthe yelled in disgust, then collected herself. "Endre wants the Empire to start a war, but Augusta is firmly against it. He couldn't persuade her to invade. But there is more than one way to start a war."

"He'll get us to strike first," Abel reasoned.

"Yes. By assassinating your pope," she whispered. "What would happen if an imperial noble killed the pope? We'd have a full-blown war in less than twenty-four hours."

"We need to inform the Vatican," Abel said.

"We can't! If word of an assassination attempt—even a failed one—becomes public knowledge, war will break out anyway."

"What should we do?" he asked.

Asthe stared intently at her companion. "I need to stop it, Abel." Her voice cracked. For her, this meant a second chance. But for Abel, he'd be defying orders and running the risk of revealing a secret pact between humans and vampires.

"I won't ask you to come with me, partner," she said.

Abel's crystal-blue eyes bore into the beautiful Methuselah. If he read her underlying meaning in calling him "partner," he didn't show it. "I can't let you do that. You have your orders, and I have mine," he said.

"So it's no use . . ." She sighed, her shoulders slumping

Cardinal Sforza had withdrawn her support of this mission, and wished Asthe to return to her homeland before any more damage was done. Asthe didn't blame Abel for obeying his superior.

"But . . ." Abel murmured, taking out his revolver. He pulled back the hammer and held out the pistol to Asthe. "If you take me hostage, then it's a different story." He smiled.

Asthe's pretty mouth stretched in a devious smile of her own.

He flipped the revolver over and pushed the grip into Asthe's hand. "Hello, Sister Kate? Can you hear me?" Abel said into his communicator.

"What is it, Father Abel? You can board now," Sister Kate replied.

"Actually, I ran into a problem. The duchess of Odessa is demanding to return to the city," Abel informed.

"Abel, I'm really busy. Flight plans, fuel plans, et cetera. Get her on the plane now. I don't care if you have to do it at gunpoint. Just get her on the ship," Sister Kate scolded.

"That's the thing. The duchess took my revolver. She has it pressed against my head. I'm a hostage. Save me, Kate," he said with absolutely no emotion.

"Abel, don't you dare pull a stunt like this. I'll get chewed out for a week if you don't get her on this ship now! Abel? Are you there?!" Sister Kate yelled.

"I really am a hostage here. No, seriously. The rest is up to you," Abel said and removed the earpiece.

"Wait! Abel—" She was cut off.

"Okay then." Abel put the communicator down. "Let's get out of here, Asthe."

"Are you sure about this?" she asked.

"No problem at all."

Asthe tilted her head, considering her partner's strange personality as she followed the smiling priest out of the terminal.

"So how are we getting back to the city? By swimming?" she asked incredulously.

The airport was on the mainland, so they had to cross the sea to get to Venice. Asthe would probably have a hard time swimming ten miles and dragging an injured priest along at the same time.

"Let's procure a boat," Abel said. He pointed to a water taxi.

The steamship's boiler had been fired up. It just sat there, docked at the port, no passengers in sight. The duo boarded. As the pulled up the mooring and Abel started flipping switches on the control panel.

"Can you drive this thing?" she asked as he fumbled with knobs. The steamship began to pull away from the dock.

"I can ride a bicycle. Does that count? Look, I'll figure something out," Abel said. "Oh . . ." Above them, the *Iron Maiden* took off. "We should have flown instead," Abel muttered.

"You said you could drive this thing!" Asthe yelled at the incompetent priest.

There was no way a slow steamship could outrun the *Iron Maiden*. They'd barely left the pier before the *Iron Maiden* was right on top of them.

"This isn't good. Sister Kate is going to beat me senseless," Abel confessed.

"Idiot! Look out!" Asthe screamed.

"Eh? Wh-whoa!" The little ship hit a marina buoy and tipped over on its side. Part of the ship's belly rose above the water as they careened into the main road's supporting wall.

Asthe shrieked as she was knocked off her feet. Both of them were thrown to the sinking side of the ship. They bumped their heads on the way down.

"Idiot! Buffoon! Moron! Twit! Turnip head!" Asthe cursed as they abandoned the steamship.

"I can barely hear you!" he yelled over the splashing waves.

They swam furiously, and pulled themselves up onto the ledge of the roadway.

"Warning! Drop your weapons and surrender yourselves. You have three seconds," boomed a mechanical voice.

Abel looked up and saw that it was Tres, amplifying his voice.

"H-hey, Tres." Abel smiled and waved at the gun Tres pointed down at him. Gunslinger's mechanical eyes coldly assessed the wet pair. "Sorry for causing a disturbance," Abel sheepishly said.

"Three, two . . ." Tres counted down.

"Whoa, whoa, stop! We'll drop our weapons! I surrender! You too, Asthe," he said.

"Idiot," she muttered. Asthe felt like a fool for getting her hopes up. She raised her hands and sighed.

Iron Maiden, this is Gunslinger. I have secured the targets. Please report the dereliction of duty by Father Nightroad to Cardinal Sforza," Tres said.

"You're going to report this to Caterina? She's going to ream me." Abel groaned.

"Get Abel *skskkksksk* . . . onboard . . . *skskskkkks* . . . problem with comm . . . *skskskss* . . . interference . . . *skskskesk,*" Sister Kate said.

Tres winced at the electronic howling. He pulled out his earpiece and reinserted it. Abel did the same.

"What's wrong?" Abel asked.

"Can't skskskksks . . . problem with *skskskskkssk* . . . contact broken, perhaps?" Sister Kate said.

Ocean spray splashed up around Abel and Asthe. The *Iron Maiden* was directly above them, engines humming, and that must have caused signal interference.

"It's the *Maiden,* she's causing our comm-links to break up," Abel said.

"Well, it *is* Terran technology, after all." Asthe snickered. She turned to regard Venice and her attitude changed. "That's it!" she screamed over the din.

"Eh? What?" Abel asked.

Asthe grabbed his shoulders and spoke quickly. "Father Abel, the second murder case at the construction company, the guy they killed, did he specialize in tide gates?! Like making dams and seawalls?!" she yelled.

"Yeah, how did you know?" Abel asked in disbelief.

"Contact Cardinal Caterina! The pope is in danger. No, all of Venice is in danger! We must evacuate all Terran in the city! The count planned to lure the pope here all along!"

"What is she talking about, Abel?" Sister Kate asked over the radio. "Caterina is visiting the tide gate as we speak."

"We have to get to her now!" Asthe yelled. "She's in mortal danger, especially if she's at the tide gate."

The red laser dot on her cheek disappeared.

"Explain," Tres commanded.

VII

Venice's nickname was "The Ocean City." But it wasn't surrounded by the ocean; it was surrounded by a shallow lagoon. A tide gate was made between the Adriatic Sea and the lagoon to control the water level and to protect the slowly sinking island. Thanks to the dam, the lagoon remained shallow, and the destructive ocean stayed at bay. However, if the seawall was compromised or broken, the ocean's water would rush in like a tsunami and flood the city. Luckily, the dam had the most advanced control system in place, but the system's weakness was that it was concentrated in one location.

Caterina bit her nails. She looked at the guards in front of the barricaded gates. They were the last line of defense for Venice. The "enemy" was the construction of the tide gate itself. It was a perfect striking point for a terrorist attack.

And as of now, it was under attack.

Without glancing at any of the side corridors, Caterina headed straight into the central control room. The gate's guards couldn't put up much of a fight, but Caterina's personal guards who'd accompanied her on this visit acted as reinforcements. It was a tenuous defense at best.

"Have you been able to contact the city?" Caterina asked.

They'd been under heavy fire. Without more men, the place would surely fall. Only half of the tide gate guards and Caterina's personal contingent could move around without limping—and most of the injuries were pretty serious. Blood trickled out of Caterina's wounded shoulder, but she seemed unfazed by it.

"The phone and radios are still disconnected," Marino Farrell, the guard leader, replied. "Your Eminence, we don't have much longer."

Marino stood before her, his square jaw trembling from fear and exhaustion. "We can secure a safe passage out with the personnel we have left. Please retreat, Your Eminence," he implored.

"I will stay. But these ladies need to go. Along with the wounded," Cardinal Caterina replied.

"But, Your Eminence!" her companion nuns objected. "We are ready to lay down our lives! But the Vatican needs Your Eminence alive . . . !" they howled.

"They are right. Please go for the sake of the Vatican," Marino begged.

"Marino, thank you, but no," Caterina said with finality. The Cardinal smiled softly and pushed away the sisters trying to treat her wound. "Even if I fall here, the Vatican will not be shaken. My successor will surely inherit my will and faith. But if I leave this seawall, what will happen to the pope in Venice?" she asked.

No one could answer her. She didn't expect them to.

Cardinal Caterina Sforza nodded calmly. Her razor-sharp eyes were filled with courage and the will to fight. "What would the world say if a cardinal ran away and left the pope and thousands of citizens behind to die? The Vatican would lose its reputation forever. I choose to remain here; I will hear no more talk of retreat," she said resolutely.

"Excellent!" A man laughed and clapped from somewhere behind them. "What commendable bravery. You really are the Woman of Steel, Cardinal Sforza. The pipsqueak pope must be delighted to find such devotion among the Vatican's top ranks," he mocked.

"One of them got in!" a guard screamed.

The nuns and guards frantically looked around for the source of the voice. The door protecting the sea gate began to vibrate. The metal bent, then twisted. It looked as though a hole had melted through its very center. A man walked through the opening and once he was through, the door resealed behind him.

"Good evening, Cardinal Sforza, Duchess of Milan. It's such a wonderful night," the stranger said.

"Who are you?" Caterina demanded.

A man in a black suit stood in front of the door. He had hip-length black hair. He looked refined, urbane even, but his mischievous smile worried her. That, and the fact that he'd just walked through a solid metal door.

"I'm a big fan of yours. I wanted to see the legendary woman of steel at least once. I'm so delighted. You are more beautiful than I'd imagined," he said.

"Stay back, you bastard!" Marino yelled.

The guards took positions around Caterina and drew their swords. The stranger smiled wickedly as they charged.

"No . . . stop!" Caterina commanded, but it was too late.

They swung wildly at him, but he easily dodged the blows. He waved his fingers in an intricate pattern and suddenly . . .

The guards froze. Their perfectly functioning eyes rolled around in terror as their bodies quit working.

"Rude little boys. Didn't you learn not to interrupt people?" he sang.

He continued to sing slowly and wistfully. It sounded like he was chanting. He placed his white-gloved hands over the guards. Pentagrams had been sewn onto the backs of the gloves.

"Zazazoo, Zazazoo, Nasatanada, Zazazoo," he sang.

The pentagram glowed in response to the chant.

The sisters screamed in horror.

The man's shadow rose up, leaving a tar-like trails. Then, a multitude of shadows ascended from the floor. They were bloated and smelled noxious, like twisted rubber dolls. Their faceless heads had only a red slit for a mouth, where fangs protruded.

"An ill-illusion?" Caterina stammered.

One of the blobs stepped forward; its slick black skin absorbed and reflected light.

"Shadow Devils," the man proclaimed. "I made some of these pets the other day for fun. As you can see, they're always so hungry. You can never feed them enough."

The shrieks they made turned everyone's blood cold.

Their heads looked like protoplasm. Even without the aid of eyes or noses, they somehow detected fresh meat. When they turned toward the frozen guards, the corners of their mouths lifted in happiness.

"No!" Caterina screamed.

The guards remained silent as they were eaten alive. The sisters' cries dissolved into unintelligible wailing.

Marino quickly pulled out his gun and took aim at the man in black.

BOOM!

The bullet bolted out of the barrel and headed straight for the mysterious man's forehead. But the man's head was not torn asunder; instead, the bullet magically found another target.

Marino's head exploded. Blood and grey matter spurted all over the room as the headless body crumpled to the ground.

"No!" Caterina yelled again.

The body collapsed on two of the nuns. Terrified, they clawed their way out from under the large corpse.

"Did you think it would be that easy?" the stranger asked. He didn't have a scratch on him.

"You . . ." Caterina glowered. The sight of Marino's headless body infuriated her. "I know who you are," she said. Her eyes

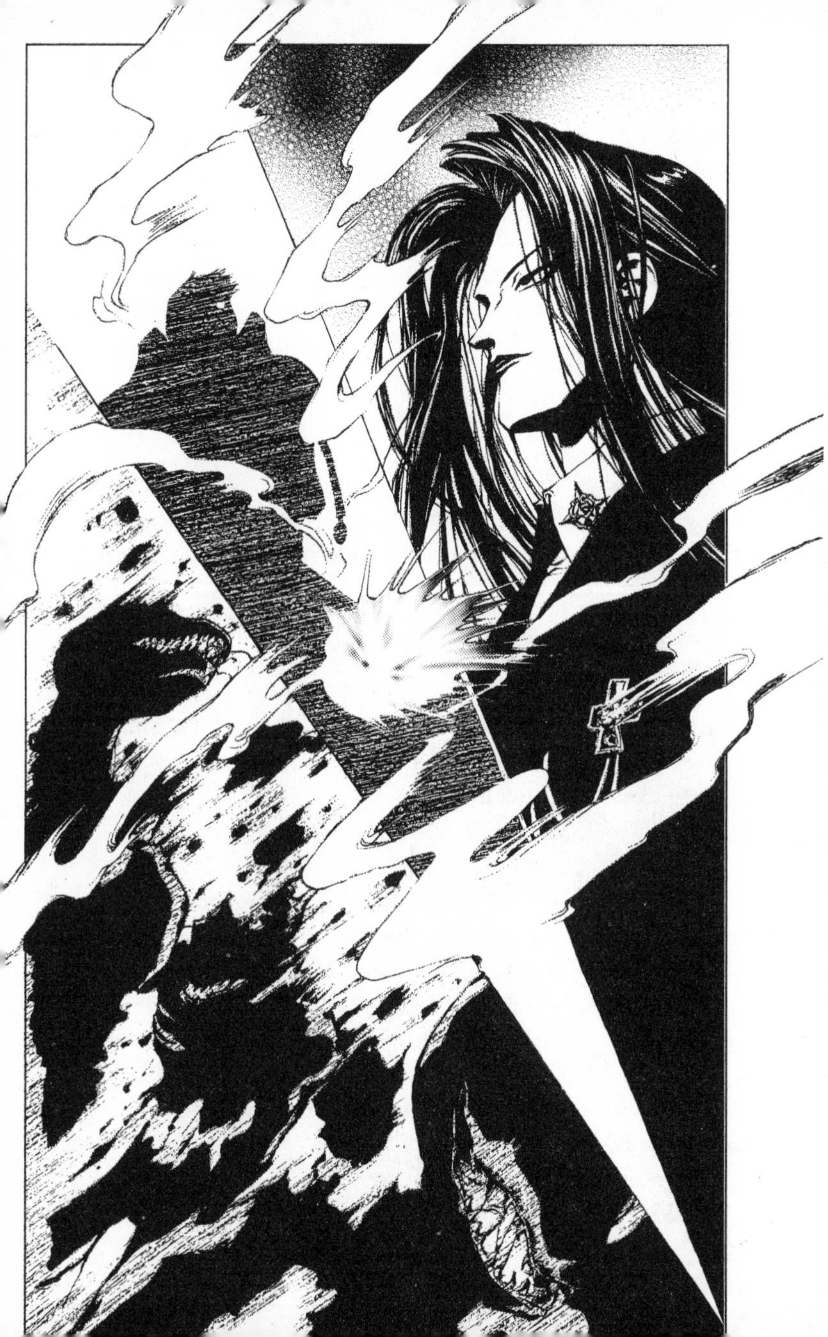

gleamed with rage. "Rosenkreuz Orden—Contra Mundi, and the ominous men who follow him . . . correct?" she spat out.

"Oh, so you know him," he said, smirking. "If you know my master, then you know there is no hope. And you really are a woman of steel to oppose us. I find that incredible. I regret that you must die. How about a deal instead? If you leave quietly and let me have this place, I will spare your life. Does that sound fair?" he asked.

"And let the pope die? That's what you're really after, isn't it?" she asked.

This time, it was Caterina's turn to smile. She pushed her blonde ringlets from her face, jingling her earrings in the process. "Even if you spared my life now, I'd die another day, fighting you. If I'm going to die anyway, I'd rather die here," she said sternly.

"Hm, you are quite intelligent. I suppose I'll deeply regret this . . ." The man snapped his fingers.

The Shadow Devils surrounding the dead guards raised their faces. They looked at the cardinal, poised for action, and the sisters who cowered behind her. The dark shadows grinned, blood dripping from their mouths.

"Will you grant me one last request?" Caterina asked.

"Of course," he responded.

"Identify yourself. I refuse to be killed by someone who hasn't even told me their name," she said.

"Oh, how rude of me," he purred. He placed a hand on his chest and bowed grandly. "My name is Kampfer. Isaak Fernand von Kampfer. Rosenkreuz Orden, Panzer Magier. I am my master's faithful servant," he said.

"Thank you, sir." She nodded and flicked her earring, grinning at her tormenter.

He nodded.

"Well then, Mister Kampfer, let me tell you something in return," she offered.

"Yes? Pretty please tell me," he said sarcastically.

"Remember this: a woman dislikes an overly talkative man. All units, open fire!" she commanded.

In that moment, the ceiling burst open.

It was a thunderous spectacle to behold. The brick and mortar of the building blew around like confetti, and streaks of metal rained down into the room. The twenty-millimeter rounds destroyed the Shadow Devils. It was an extremely well-coordinated attack, so none of the bullets hit Caterina and her group. Such marksmanship was too accurate for a normal human.

"Powerful and impressive," Kampfer purred. "But what is even more impressive is the man pulling the trigger."

Kampfer remained untouched; his suit wasn't even sullied by the falling dust. But all of his devils had been blown to smithereens. Pieces of inhuman flesh twitched and melted as stringy black ooze expanded across the floor.

"You're the one. The Gunmetal Hound owned by the Woman of Steel. The last of the ten Killing Dolls that took over the Castle of Saint Angelo five years ago." Kampfer's voice sounded delighted.

The smoke cleared, revealing an imposing figure standing protectively in front of Caterina.

"AX Agent HC-IIIX—Codename: Gunslinger," Kampfer said.

"Affirmative," Tres responded over the sound of the large Vulcan cannon hammer clanging against a firing pin.

BOOM!

VIII

nfropellium expectavit co meum et mizellium," the choirboys sang.

The opening hymn was lovely. The presiding priest swung a censer as he walked down the aisle. A line of religious officials in hooded habits entered after him. To accommodate to the size of the church, only a limited number of powerful authorities attended—the choirboys, a few guards, and the religious officials already filled up the underground chapel of Saint Mark.

"Et satin qi simul mecham contristartel concertim micsivi invini," the priest said.

While the priest recited, the pope ascended the stairs to the altar and lowered his hooded head. After a brief silence, the coffin with the holy body of Saint Mark was placed on top of the altar.

Once that was complete, the bishop of Venice read the Holy Scripture. "Lord have mercy; Christ have mercy. We live in the shadow of death and ask for forgiveness. God have mercy on us . . . Amen."

The pope stood and was escorted down the steps by one of the priests. Normally, the Eucharist would happen next, but not for this Mass. It was rumored that the pope hated giving the Sacrament and had once fainted from anxiety during the ritual. In the peculiar silence, the young pope moved toward the door.

"Alessandro XVIII, three hundred ninety-ninth Pope of the Vatican—I came to see you!" a voice roared. The voice belonged to a small boy.

The crowd focused their attention on one of the choirboys who had risen to his feet.

From underneath his ornate smock, he produced an axe. "I am Endre—Count of Zagrev! You are but a lowly ape that dares to oppose me! I shall have your head!" he screamed.

The pope's guards were the best soldiers in the world. They all drew guns and on the assailant, but their human brains could not catch up to a Methuselah's speed. The count went into haste mode, jumped over the astonished crowd, and brought the axe down onto the motionless pope.

KLANG!

Endre's axe ricocheted off the helpless victim and he went flying into a stained glass window. His face was covered with mosaic glass. He sneered in disgust.

"You're not the pope!" he screamed.

The pope's hood fell back. A woman with ivory hair held a thick saber above her head.

The count, recognizing her brass-colored eyes, gaped. "Astharoshe Asran! How?" Endre squealed.

"Endre Kourza, in the name of the Father, the Son, and Holy Spirit, you are under arrest for four counts of murder," said the bishop of Venice. The bishop, or rather, the man impersonating him, pushed thick glasses up his nose.

"Resistance is futile. Surrender!" Asthe yelled.

"How did you find me so quickly?! Where is the real pope?" Endre demanded.

Abel cleared his throat and held up a finger as if he were about to lecture an unruly student. "We found a memo inside Marco Colleoni's safe. You took his daughter hostage, so he faked the authentication of Saint Mark's holy body for her return. Once we discovered that, we sent the pope home. The Mass was canceled. The priests here are all members of AX Agency. I strongly suggest that you drop your weapon and surrender," Abel said.

"A relative found the memo when they were sorting through the family will," Asthe continued. "If you hadn't killed so excessively, we would have never known. But your bloodlust was your downfall. You cannot get away this time."

The priests pulled rifles from under their robes. In eerie unison, they cocked their weapons.

Endre snickered, then laughed. "Surrender?! I don't think so, little girl."

Asthe grabbed Abel. "Duck!"

The count's axe landed right where Abel's head had been. "You want a piece of me, Astharoshe? Come and get it!" Endre screamed.

The old vampire snatched up one of the choirboys and took cover. Asthe chased after him.

"Protect the children!" Abel yelled to the AX agents.

Endre jumped on top of the fake remains and hit a secret switch on the base of the altar. The pedestal, weighing almost a ton, fell through a trapdoor that led to a secret chamber beneath the underground chapel. It fell several yards into an Armageddon tunnel—an escape route designed to hide people when Armageddon came—and Endre rode atop the coffin with the choirboy in his grasp.

"You're not getting away!" Asthe shouted.

The tunnel, lined with reflective paint, glowed an eerie white. The shadows of the Methuselah running through the white space in haste mode were too blurry for the naked human eye.

Asthe gained slight ground. "It's over, Endre!" she yelled. She struck her sword at the boyish vampire's back, aiming to avoid the child in his arms.

KLANG!

"What?" Asthe said, befuddled.

Before the sword could reach her foe, it was deflected. Eight silver orbs were orbiting the vampire as he fled.

"Aegis shield!" she lamented.

"Drop your weapon, Duchess of Odessa!" Pointing his sharp fingernails at the now-unconscious boy's throat, Endre turned around and dropped out of haste mode. "This is the second time, Astharoshe. No, if I count the time I slaughtered your partner, that would make it three times, right? If you want to spare the boy's life, throw down your sword," he said.

Rage burned deep inside her. She was almost blinded by it; the faces of the dead echoed in her mind's eye. It didn't take long for Asthe to make the decision to drop her sword.

"How dare you interrupt me during my finest hour? You will pay for that," Endre growled. He picked the sword up off the stone floor, and then licked sharp blade. "This wasn't my only plan, little girl. It was merely the most direct method. Still, the pope *will* die— eventually. I've made arrangements for that already." He cackled.

"If you're talking about the tide gate, others have taken care of that. This city will not drown." She smiled.

"Hah! So you knew about that too!" he exclaimed, impressed. "Well, well; I guess I underestimated a little girl like you. But it ends here. The punishment for interfering with my grand schemes is quite severe, Astharoshe." He glowered.

"Endre, you're wrong on two counts. First, it doesn't end here, but you're too stupid to know it," she hissed. "And your grand scheme? It's crap, you perverted freak. You should stop boasting about ideas you can't make real!"

It had been a long time since anyone had dared to speak to Endre that way. After all, he was vampire nobility. *Criminally insane* vampire nobility. "What did you say to me?" he stammered.

Asthe continued to lambaste him. "You're such an insolent coward and so full of crap. On top of that, you kill the Terran for fun, like a barbarian, but you pretend to be a sophisticated aristocrat. You're not cultured. You're a hillbilly on a power trip. You perverted freak; how can your little brain come up with grand schemes? Don't make me laugh. I'm embarrassed to even talk to trash like you," Asthe said.

His angelic face went white for a moment, then reddened, and finally turned blue.

"You little bitch!" Endre screamed.

The silver aegis orbs clanked to the ground. The old vampire raised his sword. "What do *you* know? I'm different! I'm not like the others! They didn't accept me! That's why I—!" he bellowed and then stopped short, embarrassed.

He aimed straight at Asthe's heart and then launched himself forward. "Die, bitch!"

The echo of gunfire throughout the tunnel wasn't that loud, but the bullets were enough in number to drop the boyish vampire in mid-flight.

Endre's body bent like a boomerang; first he slammed against the wall, then bounced along the floor. Grabbing his stomach, the count squirmed and shook. A silver bullet—a weapon all Methuselah despise—had burrowed through his abdomen and lodged into his spine.

"Terran . . . ! You fooled me!" Endre yelled at the silver-haired priest standing behind Asthe.

"I didn't think he'd fall for such a lame trick," Asthe said as she collected the aegis orbs on the ground.

The one problem with that defense system was that the protective shield prevented the user from attacking. It was a fatal flaw. "Good job, Father."

Abel was panting. He rested his hands on his knees as he tried to catch his breath. "You made me sweat a little. You guys were way ahead of me," he joked. "And we might have discussed our plan beforehand. I'm not such a good marksman, you know."

His facial expression was so funny that Asthe cracked up. "Well, I was really worried about you, partner!"

"There you go again, saying 'partner' whenever it suits you." Abel paused, then blinked adorably. "Hey! This is the first time I've seen you laugh, Asthe. You're so beautiful." He'd just blurted it out; it sounded so sincere, almost worshipful.

"Idiot," she replied, unable to hide her blush.

Mission accomplished. She just had to take Endre back to her homeland. She could finally leave this damned country. Everyone in the Empire would embrace her as she returned in triumph.

But . . .

"Thank you for everything, Abel," she said softly.

"You're welcome." He bowed, looking as goofy as ever.

Asthe squinted at him. She probably wouldn't ever see him again. As a Terran, he would probably live for only another fifty years. Asthe studied him intently so as to remember his face. For Asthe—who would live at least three hundred more years—fifty years was nothing. Even if she stepped into the Outers' world again later, she probably wouldn't recognize his aged face.

"Please remember me," she requested. "I won't remember any faces of the lowly and feeble Terran. That's why you need to call out for me, next time we meet, okay? One day, when the Empire takes over the world, I'll hire you to remove fleas from my cat or something."

"I look forward to that," Abel said, his eyes twinkling. He smiled as he reached for her. He stroked his thumb over her fingers, and then brought the back of her delicate hand up to his lips for a chaste kiss.

IX

Clear. Rewriting combat mode from genocide to search and destroy," Tres said.

Kampfer was nowhere to be found among the rubble. He might have been blown to bits by the three hundred rounds of twenty-millimeter bullets, but the AX agents kept looking. His remains needed to be examined for any clues or connections to the other terrorists.

"Damage report, Cardinal Sforza," Tres asked.

"I'm fine. Good job, Father Tres," Caterina replied.

Tres bowed to his mistress. He dropped his spent mini-cannon to the floor. For now, evacuating the survivors came before the search for Kampfer.

"The *Iron Maiden* is airborne and standing by. Cardinal Sforza, we request immediate departure as soon as possible," Tres informed.

"Have the nuns board before me. How is the pope doing?" Caterina asked.

"Crusnik and the duchess of Odessa were deployed. Once the target appears, they are to track and destroy him," Tres responded.

"Wonderful! Great job, AX Agents." Everyone except Tres turned to find the source of the deliberately mocking applause.

"Y-you're . . ." Caterina stammered.

"How rude of your windup toy not to greet me first. My suit is so dirty now," Kampfer chided, combing his hands through his long black hair. His handsome face was spotless.

"Father Tres. Add to your report. The Count of Zagrev has been arrested," Abel piped in over the radio.

BOOM! BOOM!

Tres, with his back still turned to Kampfer, fired. The Jericho M13 was aimed right at Kampfer's forehead. The two shots should have hit him square in the face, but . . .

"A useless toy. So barbaric," Kampfer murmured in disgust.

Kampfer stared at the two bullets floating in midair. He raised his hand and the bullets clanked to the floor. "Father Tres, you are very talented, but you still don't understand the meaning of killing. Let me teach you," Kampfer said.

The pentagram embroidered on the magician's white glove started to glow red. "In front of me Youngs, behind me Teletarkae, in my right hand a sword, in my left hand a shield, around me the Pentagram glows, and in the stone, the Star of David is placed . . . come to me, Sword of Beelzebub," he sang.

Kampfer lightly flicked his wrist, and the trembling nun next to Caterina lost her head.

"Sister Anna!" Caterina screamed.

Sister Anna's young face, her eyes opened wide, rolled to the feet of Sister Rachel.

"No!" Rachel screamed.

"Please don't move, Sister Rachel," Tres warned.

But she'd gone into shock. Ignoring Father Tres' warning, she stumbled toward the exit.

His back still turned, Kampfer smiled. With another flick of his wrist, Sister Rachel split into four pieces. She collapsed like a broken mannequin, her organs spewing out.

The remaining sisters were speechless. All they could do was to cling to the pale-faced Caterina.

"It was Syrus who said, 'The fear of death is worse than death itself.' Don't move, Father Tres. Killing Dolls are no fun. You don't have emotions, do you?" Kampfer asked.

Kampfer flexed his fingers.

"There's no fun in killing a puppet. You won't scream, or cry, or beg. That's not amusing. Why don't you learn how to be cute like these girls?" Kampfer asked.

"Negative. No time," Tres responded. Looking down at the dead bodies, something changed in his typically monotonous voice. "Three hundred seconds before more reinforcements arrive. I must terminate you before that. No time to waste."

"Oh really?" Kampfer adjusted his gloves. "You're going to terminate me, right?"

"Affirmative," Tres said, scanning the area. He looked at Caterina, the trembling sisters, and the dead bodies on the floor. "I will destroy you—and leave no bones."

"Try it." Kampfer's fingers twitched. He pointed at his enemy, but Tres was no longer there. Instead, a trail of dust streaked through the air.

An invisible sword zoomed after Tres, hurtling upward, tearing a gaping hole in the ceiling.

"You're fast. But is that all you've got?" Kampfer asked. His fingers wriggled like a spider's legs. It looked like he was playing the piano; the cracks in the walls increased.

In the next instant, the force of the invisible weapon caught up to the priest's chin.

"It's over, Gunslinger," Kampfer spat.

"I was .03 seconds too late," Tres admitted as his right arm broke. The hand holding his pistol snapped off at the wrist. A thick nozzle hung from his wrist cavity. Thousand-degree magnesium flames abruptly blasted out of it. In the bluish-white fire, a few strands of Kampfer's long black hair turned gray and then disintegrated.

"Mono-carbon fiber!" Caterina yelled under her breath.

Mono-carbon fiber was one of the lost technologies from before the Armageddon. It was made up of several C60 carbon molecules—the thinnest and strongest fiber ever made. Though it was vulnerable to fire, the fiber could cut the toughest diamond, and depending on how it was used, it doubled as the deadliest of weapons.

Under Tres' fiery assault, the Sword of Beelzebub turned to ash.

"You figured it out. You're pretty good, Gunslinger. But you're still just a doll." Kampfer grinned.

Tres pointed his M13 at Kampfer. The laser sights accurately aimed at Kampfer's forehead. But even the M13's 513 Maxima round couldn't penetrate Kampfer's shield. If he fired, the round would have ricocheted back toward his own head.

As Kampfer laughed, Tres fired twice. Two brass bullets sliced through the air.

Kampfer sighed, bored. "It's no use. You can't hit me."

"They'll find their target," Tres replied.

They were both correct.

Kampfer employed The Shield of Asmoday. The bullets deflected off the power shield, spinning exactly 180 degrees. The rounds barely missed the priest as he ducked. They went farther behind Tres and hit a metal firewall at a shallow angle. Once again, they ricocheted. Finally, they deflected off a dead guard's sword and bounced back toward Kampfer.

Both of his gloved hands were blown off. He looked down in disbelief. "Unbelievable," was all he said. *How could the Killing Doll have calculated the ricochet angle after it hit the shield?*

"I suppose the name Gunslinger fits you well. Just like I am rightfully called Wizard," Kampfer said.

Wizard seemed to shrink as he sank into the floor. "Don't even think about following me, you puppet," Kampfer said to Tres. Looking one last time at Tres and Caterina, he was swallowed by his own shadow. "I will probably see you again in the near future. When the ring of fate closes, you will become my great sacrifices," he said.

Caterina blinked rapidly. Now, only Kampfer's head remained outside his shadow.

"What are you doing?! Shoot him, Gunslinger!" she yelled.

Tres raised his arms, trying to obey his mistress, but he stopped suddenly.

"Fa-Father Tres!" Caterina screamed.

Both of Tres' arms were severed at the shoulders. They fell heavily to the floor. Caterina couldn't believe what she saw: Tres dropping to his knees, fluids streaming from his wounds.

"This makes us even. No grudges, Father Tres. Farewell," Kampfer said. His laughter echoed even after he sank completely into his shadow.

✝

"The Count of Zagrev has been taken into custody and is being transported. He will probably arrive in a day or so," Asthe said, kneeling.

"Good job, Duchess." The obscured image of Augusta, Empress of the New Human Empire, looked down from her floating throne. Her electronically altered voice vibrated throughout in the royal chambers. "Duchess of Odessa, you mentioned a collaborator from the Outer World. How was he?" the empress asked.

"What do you mean by that, Empress?" Asthe responded with a question of her own.

Augusta noticed that her shoulders quivered momentarily. "I'm asking if he was helpful. You expressed favorable thoughts about him in the report, no?"

"N-no! Just that, for a Terran, he was useful. If you wish, shall I add m-more details to the r-report?" Asthe stammered.

"No, that's not necessary. I do not want to burden you with any more work. Excellent job. You are dismissed," Augusta said finally.

"Yes, Your Highness! As you wish." Asthe bowed.

Once the tall duchess of Odessa left the royal chambers, the lonely room's soft lights grew stronger, illuminating the small figure of a young girl. She stretched out and spoke in her real voice. "So he's still on the humans' side? Then maybe I shouldn't pick a fight with the Vatican. One of him, we could overcome . . . but two of them? That would be troublesome."

A green-eyed teenager sat on the throne. Her bobbed brunette hair trimmed her pretty face; she had long, skinny arms and legs; her energetic expression was cat-like in nature. The girl, Empress Augusta Vradica, took off her large hat and draped herself across her floating throne.

"He sure hasn't changed. He's still honoring his lost lover's wish and siding with the Terran. I don't understand it, but somehow he's popular with the girls. He needs to take a new lover already. I highly recommend Astharoshe. If I was a boy, I'd go after her for sure," Augusta said.

The royal chamber's interior design depicted a Canadian landscape before the Armageddon: a nostalgic, lush green forest. The smell of chlorophyll and the chirping birds were soothing.

"Oh, what should I do?" The little girl sighed. Eventually, she fell into a restful sleep. A small songbird perched on her chest, which rose and fell in a gentle rhythm.

✝

"I've come for you, Count," Kampfer whispered.

"Ooh, Kampfer!" Endre squeaked.

The boyish vampire scrambled and looked at the man on the other side of the bars. The guards were nowhere to be seen.

"Thank you! Thank you, Kampfer," he whispered.

"You're welcome, Count. Will you join me on the upper deck? I have an aircraft waiting for you."

"By all means," Endre said with a wicked smile.

They left the boathouse's cell together. Endre scanned the area. The guard ship was supposed to have over fifty passengers, but it was dead quiet.

"What happened to the crew?" Endre asked.

Kampfer just shrugged his shoulders.

Endre was slightly irked at the Terran's nonchalant response, but thought better than to question his good fortune. If he'd been transported back to the Empire, then he would have gotten a punishment worse than death. At least Kampfer was helping him escape.

His stomach growled. He started to thirst. He didn't have too many options. Even a child or old man would suffice, but there was no prey aboard the ship but Kampfer. *Shall I eat him?* Endre pondered. He smiled as he approached Kampfer from behind. *Come to think of it, I have no more use for Wizard.*

The count would have to go into hiding for quite some time. It would be advantageous for him to eliminate anyone who knew him. Wizard could be very useful in various situations, but he was a liability.

"By the way, Count . . ." Kampfer said, as if he'd read the count's mind. "Congratulations. You gave a great show."

"What are you talking about?" Endre demanded.

"The incident in Venice, of course. That was quite a success," Kampfer said.

"Do not mock me, you Terran dog!" Endre yelled.

But Kampfer, with his back facing the elderly vampire, shook his head.

"Mock you? Of course not. The plan *was* quite successful. The Empire and the Vatican were able to create an alliance. This is good news," Kampfer said.

"Wh-what do you mean by that?" Endre stammered.

"You can't destroy that which does not exist, right? This incident helped them to create an alliance. Even a perverted freak like you—who could only kill the infirm—was quite useful. We just needed to put you in the right situation," Kampfer said.

"You insolent fool!" Endre shouted. His young, pretty face contorted. "Terran! How dare you?!" The count snarled, baring his fangs and claws. He lunged, but the ancient vampire only grabbed thin air.

Suddenly, he started to sink. "Wha—?" Endre started. His legs were sinking into Kampfer's shadow, as if he were being pulled down by tar or quicksand. "M-my legs . . . !" he squeaked.

Kampfer, looking over his shoulder with mild interest, lit a cigar. "It's trouble to have a weasel like you stirring things up later. The stage needs to be cleared of clutter before the main actor can make an entrance."

"What *are* you?" Endre demanded, already sunken down to his chest. "Kampfer! Why?"

His face sank completely into the dark pool, until only his hand stuck out. He desperately tried to grab something, anything, but eventually he was consumed.

"What a magnificent moon," Kampfer sighed.

He looked up to the skies as if nothing had happened. In the southern hemisphere, a full moon hung next to a smaller, irregularly shaped "vampire moon."

"When the world ends, it'll probably be on a pretty night like this. And it will happen soon. What a beautiful night that will be," he said.

Wizard threw his cigar into the ocean, stuck his hands in his pocket, and walked into the darkness.

SWORD DANCER

*Appoint a way, that a sword may come to Rab'bath
of the Ammonites and to Judah in Jerusalem the defense.*
—Ezekiel 21:20

From my initial inspection, there are no outstanding issues with Tres being treated in Milan. There are no virus infections in his main processors. He should be able to recover in about a month," the elderly man said.

Palazzio Spada, otherwise known as the Foreign Affairs office, was quieter than usual. The thin-faced man threw a thick file onto the desk and tapped his cheek. He smiled confidently and played with the unlit pipe in his mouth.

"I can go to Milan as early as tomorrow. We're off for our semester break. The students have ample homework to keep them busy. What do you think, Your Eminence?" he asked.

"I'll leave the recovery of Father Tres to you, Professor," said Cardinal Caterina Sforza. She rested her elbows on her desk and sighed deeply. A slight furrow of her brows was all that indicated her very real concerns. "We don't have enough AX agents as it is. I look forward to his quick recovery."

"Leave it to me, Your Eminence. I'll finish this before my college classes start."

If this world had picture of supreme confidence, then it would be a portrait of the "Professor," otherwise known as Doctor William W. Wordsworth. He pulled out a match from under his priest's robe and was about to light his pipe, when suddenly a nun's hologram appeared before him.

"Good evening, Professor Wordsworth. This is a nonsmoking area. Please smoke in the hall or on the balcony."

"Oh, excuse me . . . My, but you are a beautiful woman, Sister Kate."

"Thank you for your compliment. But you still cannot smoke here," the nun said gently, silently scolding the Professor with her eyes.

He removed the pipe from his mouth.

"I am back, Cardinal," Sister Kate said. "As you ordered, I have dispatched the unit in Amsterdam. He is planning on conducting the mission tonight."

Caterina nodded. "Good job, Sister Kate. Continue the liaison."

"Hmm, Amsterdam, eh . . . ? Oh, is this about the incident at Oude Kerk?" the Professor asked in that nasal voice of his. He made circles with his right index finger on his temple, and bit his unlit pipe. "The murders and blood extortion of the bishop and several religious personnel . . . So, who did you send?"

"The Four-City Alliance, including Amsterdam, is a very sensitive region. Therefore, I deployed the agent most familiar with the location."

"So you sent Sword Dancer? Hmm, are you sure about that?"

Caterina eyed the man carefully.

Sister Kate saw the Professor's expression turn sour, so she asked, "Is there a problem with that, Professor?"

Caterina said, "He was born in Antwerp and is familiar with the area. And I think he is capable of the job. Is something wrong?"

"Therein lies the problem. It is a complex situation." The Professor pondered for a moment, then turned to Caterina. "You are aware of how he became an AX agent, Your Eminence. I can't help but think that he is not the best choice for this case."

Caterina sighed and stood up. "There *is* no other choice."

She went to window and looked down at the nightscape. For the past few days, this winter hadn't been as cold as in previous years, but tonight, it started to turn chilly again. The streets were quiet; only stray dogs and shadows milled about.

"I don't have enough AX agents—hardly any, actually. So if he gets out of control, then . . ." Caterina spoke to her reflection in the window. "I need help to stop him. Professor, could you please go to Milan as soon as possible?"

I

After turning at the third intersection, the footsteps dogging the young girl grew louder. Sister Agnes couldn't stand it any longer—she broke out into a sprint. The nun's robe, dripping wet, clung to her thin legs.

Just who is that, anyway?! she thought. Agnes recalled the mysterious shadow she'd glimpsed behind her and shuddered.

When she'd left the police station, she hadn't noticed anyone behind her. She'd heard footsteps following her when she'd entered a desolate area just past the embankment. Whoever followed her was keeping their distance, but continued hunting her around every corner.

That night in Amsterdam was as quiet as a tomb.

The port city, lower than the sea level, was protected by seawalls. On a chilly night like this, fog from the canals covered the streets with white mist. Of course, most people wouldn't dare to venture out on a night like this. Even Agnes wouldn't have gone out. She'd locked herself in her room at the church, content to spend the evening indoors, but then she'd been called to the police station.

Now there was nobody to ask for help and she was running out of breath . . . Thankfully, she noticed a small boat was parked at the edge of the canal.

It was a gondola with a covered carriage, something that a noble would use for discreet encounters. She didn't want to use it without permission, but there wasn't anyone around. When she got to the canal, she jumped on board.

About ten seconds after Agnes had hidden in the gondola's cabin, the shadow came out of the fog. He wore a dark cloak like that of an undertaker; the hood covered his face. Even more disturbing was the sight of a long metal staff bound to his back. The staff was about as tall as Agnes. It was suspicious to carry around such a large thing anyhow.

The stalker stopped beside the boat. His target had disappeared. He tilted his head to the side, then looked around like a hunting dog that had lost its prey.

"God, please help me . . . oh God . . ." Agnes tried to suppress her trembling. She clutched her rosary. As her stalker looked toward the boat, his green eyes glowed faintly from under the hood. Their eyes met . . .

He looked away.

As if nothing had ever happened, the stalker turned and strode in the opposite direction. His heavy footsteps melted into the fog and eventually all traces of him disappeared.

"Phew." Agnes took a deep breath and got out of the gondola. "I wonder who he was, anyway?"

But deep down, she had an inkling.

One week after the tragedy, she'd sensed someone watching her whenever she went out. That man had probably been stalking her all this time.

Agnes, close to tears, went back into the streets. She patted off her wet skirt. *I'll go back to the church. There's nobody there, but at least I'll be protected by the thick walls and tall gate . . .*

The girl almost slipped and fell. It was a blessing, for she'd been about to walk right into a horse-drawn carriage that had been hidden in the fog.

"Please be careful, young lady. It's dangerous to be out on a foggy night," a chilling voice warned her. "Oh? Are you perhaps

Sister Agnes? What a coincidence. I was actually looking for you. This is great."

A young man standing on the gangway of the carriage laughed sarcastically. Clad in expensive black clothing and a blue satin cape, he looked like a typical noble—like one of the wealthy merchants who controlled the Four-City Alliance. He had a golden rapier hanging from his hip, a sapphire floral ring, and a gentlemanly stature.

Agnes stepped back immediately. She noticed fangs poking out from the edge of his thin lips.

"Ah! What?" The nun tried to distance herself from the carriage, but black-clothed men blocked her retreat.

"Don't be so afraid, little girl. I've no plans to eat you, for crying out loud."

One of the smaller men with snakelike eyes cackled. "Sir Peter wanted to ask you a few questions about the priest killings that happened last week, that's all. Why don't you come with us?"

"I-I don't know anything," the nun stuttered. She shivered and her teeth chattered. "When I came back, everyone was killed. Please believe me! I really didn't see anything!"

"Oh, are you sure about that? But you are the only survivor. I have more questions for you. Please come with us." The gentleman, smiling wryly, extended his long arm.

Agnes noticed the claws. Jerking back, she yelled, "D-don't get near me, you monster!"

"Monster?" The gentleman's face hardened. *"Monster?* Are you calling *me* a monster?" His change in tone frightened her even more.

One of the men in black approached and whispered, "Please calm down, Sir Peter. Your brother requested that you bring the girl back alive—"

"Don't talk to me, you stinking Terran!" Sir Peter swung his thin arm, and the black-clothed man flew out to the edge of the street. Without so much as a glance toward his immobile subordinate, the gentleman grabbed Agnes' shoulders with his clawed hands. "How could a useless critter like you call me a monster? Such bravado, for a mere girl . . ."

He gnashed his teeth, which sounded like grinding metal, and his claws dug into the nun's white flesh. The vampire slowly inched his face toward the suffering girl's. His curved fangs extended from his poisonous mouth. His pointed tongue stuck out; he licked the neck of his prey—

The next instant, the monster arched back, covered his face, and cried out in agony.

"Sir Peter?!" his men shouted.

Agnes had been thrown onto the cobblestone street. Ignoring her completely, the black-clothed men noticed a small dagger, the size of a toothpick, piercing the groaning vampire's tongue.

While the rest looked at their wounded master, one of the smaller men turned to the direction the dagger had flown from and asked, "Who the hell are you?!"

A man in a dark, black robe stood on the other side of the street. Underneath his covered hood, green eyes glowed. A long staff was bound to his back.

"Get away from the girl, vampire," he said, addressing Sir Peter. "I'm sure I will introduce myself to you soon, but right now I would like to tend to the girl's wounds. Please just go away. If you decide not to comply . . . then I will kill you," the strange man said.

"Kill? Is the man *sane* to think that he could kill a vampire—the strongest creature on Earth?!" Sir Peter, covering his bloody mouth, screamed in retort. "Don't kid yourself, you fool!"

He pulled the shining silver dagger out of his tongue and pushed aside his subordinate.

"*Kill? Kill me?* I don't know who the hell you are, but stop this farce!" The small dagger swished in the air, flying almost faster than the speed of sound, back at its owner's face.

But instead of wounding the stranger, the vampire and the black-clothed men gasped in surprise.

The man dodged slightly and smacked the dagger away. "What?!"

"It's no use—you cannot kill me," the man said softly, his long staff held out in front of him.

"Hmm, so you were able to dodge that . . . You're pretty good, for a Terran," said the Methuselah. He lewdly licked his lips and drew the rapier from its scabbard at his hip.

"All right! Then how about this?!"

By the time the sword was completely drawn out, the vampire had already lunged forward. A normal human would not have been able to follow the speed of such an action with their eyes.

But the strange man was unafraid. Instead, he pulled back his metal staff, resting it beside his left hip, and then he bent his knees slightly.

"Stupid Terran! You think you can stop me with that thing?!" Sir Peter spouted, bringing up his blade.

The thin sword was made of Omega Titanium—the finest synthesized metal. Add to that a Methuselah's strength and speed, and a metal staff would be shredded like thin paper.

Sir Peter saw the man's cape float up without the aid of any wind. It struck him as odd.

Their shadows overlapped. The sound of clanging metal rang throughout the night.

"I wanted to know your name before I kill you, you piece of filth!" Sir Peter shouted shrilly, his blade swinging sharply.

He heard a low voice whisper, "Hugue."

I surely sliced him, so why is he still talking? Sir Peter thought.

He was supposed to be running past the man, but instead, he was looking at the Terran's back, upside down. "Huh?"

The slashed black cape fell down from the stranger's shoulder. But, when the man turned around . . . The last thing the vampire saw was the man's sad, handsome face and his pale blond hair tucked under the hood.

The young man in a priest's robe spoke softly. "My name is Hugue. Father Hugue."

Sir Peter finally realized that he was not hanging upside down. In actuality, his throat had been slashed so deeply that his head was barely hanging by a thin strip of skin. Eventually, the weight of his head caused the skin to break, and he fell to the ground with a sickening *squish*.

✝

"I really don't know a thing about the incident at Oude Kerk!" Count of Amsterdam Carrel van der Verf snarled in the darkness. His crooked nose oozed sweat. "I really don't know. None of our clan members touched Old Church!"

"Which means, Carrel . . ."

Three holograms surrounded the blue-suited Methuselah. To the right, a young man wearing a red tuxedo smiled menacingly, like a cat with a cornered mouse. "Which means that you are foolish. You let a drifter slip through your town without your knowledge . . . It's such a disgrace that you call yourself one of the Count Four, really."

Carrel glared at the young man who was now toying with his curly light brown hair. "Shut up, Memlink. Who do you think you're talking to? Keep going on like that, and I'll kill you!" barked Carrel.

"Kill me? Kill Hans Memlink? Too funny. Come to Antwerp any time. I'll welcome you. Shall we decide the date of our duel?"

"Stop it, both of you!" an old gentleman in black, in the center, said to the bickering Methuselah. His hair was graying, but his thick eyebrows were jet-black. His eagle eyes suited his thin lips. He looked severe, strict. The old gentleman—Count of Brussels Tierry Darsus—scolded the young men. "Think about our dire situation! A church was attacked in our territory. Do you gentlemen understand the meaning of all this?"

"The count of Brussels is absolutely right. We don't have time to squabble among ourselves." Next to the old gentleman was a young man wearing a white suit, nodding solemnly. His slightly slender build made him look like an accountant. But behind his silver glasses, his eyes were sharp, clever.

The young man, Count of Bruges Gie de Grandville, gloomily voiced his opinion:

"We must find the killer as soon as possible and take care of this matter once and for all. Count of Amsterdam, is it possible that Methuselah who aren't a part of the Count Four are lurking in the cities?"

"No," Carrel quickly replied.

Count Four was the alias for the group of Methuselah that worked in the Four-City Alliance's underground.

Ten years ago, the Count Four conglomerate quickly gained strength, destroyed and absorbed criminal organizations of Terran and other Methuselah clans, and eventually gained control of the Four-City Alliance's underworld. It was close to impossible to have an unknown Methuselah drift through town without Carrel's knowledge.

"For example, is it possible that one of the Istavans run by the count of Hungary or the Regas run by the count of Courant have come through town?" Darsus raised his eyebrows, questioning the men.

"The Four-City Alliance is inside the Terran's realm. The reason we survived is because we never touched their churches. But the Alliance government won't be the only organization coming for us. Those other folks will surely get involved," said Gie.

"Those other folks?" asked Carrel.

"The religious fanatics touting nonsense about protecting the Terran—the group of killers aiming to spoil our plans." Gie sounded poetic as he spoke.

Memlink stopped playing with his brown hair and interjected in a high-pitched voice, "Vatican! Those killers! What mess did we just get into?!"

"Stop it, Memlink. We don't have time to squabble," Darsus, a grandfatherly figure, scolded, then turned to Carrel. "Anyway, the three of us will put pressure on the Alliance government to prevent the Vatican from getting involved. Meanwhile, Carrel, find the killer in any way possible."

"Okay . . . I'm currently looking for the nun that survived. I'll get the details from her," Carrel said.

"Roger. But you know that you need to do this quickly. We don't have much time," warned Darsus, glaring.

The hologram of Darsus flickered. The figure slowly lost its illumination and faded away. Moments after, the hologram of the man in the red tuxedo faded as well.

Carrel spoke to the remaining Methuselah in a low voice. "What's wrong, Gie? Do you have something else to say?"

"Yes. I'm a little concerned about something," Gie said. The thin Methuselah pushed up his glasses and stared back at Carrel intently. There was a brief moment of silence, possibly out of respect.

Carrel, losing his patience, broke in. "What are you concerned about?"

"Everything about this incident is disturbing. Don't you find it suspicious? Religious personnel were found killed heinously by a Methuselah in your town. Because of that, the possibility of the Vatican getting involved is rather high, and the status of the Count Four is being threatened . . . Isn't this sequence of events almost too perfect?"

"Hmm, now that you put it that way . . ." Carrel rubbed his crooked nose. He was known for his warrior skills, but he wasn't too bright. However, even *he* felt there was something strange about these incidents.

One week ago, ten religious personnel were killed in Amsterdam's Oude Kerk—that much he knew. The cervical vertebrae of all the victims were snapped, and vampire bite marks were on their necks. It was obviously a Methuselah attack.

But, as he'd just stated, the chances of it being an attack by a Methuselah who simply drifted into town was low. Also, Count of Amsterdam's clan members, including his younger brother Peter, were loyal to Carrel. They wouldn't do something so reckless.

So that left . . .

"A traitor in a different clan?" Carrel guessed.

"You cannot rule it out. But, if there is someone in the Count Four who wants to take you down, then the pieces fit together," said Gie.

"Traitor . . . Memlink?!" Carrel pounded the mahogany desk in a fit of rage. "That's right; why didn't I think of it earlier?"

Amsterdam was the second wealthiest city, after Brussels. If someone were able to remove Carrel, then that person could become quite powerful. After that, it would be easy to take over the Count Four if they so desired.

But the elderly Darsus and the newcomer, Gie, wouldn't dream of such plot. Gie hadn't forgotten the debt he owed to Carrel, so he supported Carrel in this way; and though Darsus was infamous for his fearful, atrocious nature, he had weakened with age and usually avoided trouble.

But, Memlink of Antwerp—he was different. He acted like an aristocrat, spending lots of money to gather pieces of art, beautiful women, and pretty young boys; he'd been outspoken about his envy of Amsterdam's riches. On top of that, Memlink had loathed Carrel ever since Carrel had refused to lend him some money. *That fool probably wouldn't care if he pulled in the Vatican to get his way.*

"There is no proof. Regardless, Count of Amsterdam, you should beware," warned Gie.

"I know. But he'd better watch out as well. Thanks, Gie. I won't forget your deeds," replied Carrel.

The skinny count of Bruges smiled back sincerely. "My pleasure, sire. With Count Darsus weakening in his old age, you are the pillar of the Count Four, and I owe you my allegiance for letting me fill one of this group's vacant seats."

"Pillar? Me?" Carrel happily rubbed the side of his nose, but concern tightened his face. *Well, it's nice to be complimented, but now isn't the time to revel in it. I must figure out a way to deal with Memlink before he makes his next move.* "Thanks, Gie. Once this is taken care of, I'll visit you. Maybe we can go hunting or something."

"I eagerly await the opportunity," Gie said. As the bowing figure of the young Methuselah faded out, the chandelier above turned on. In the center of the lit library, Carrel stretched his legs onto the mahogany desk and folded his thick arms across his chest.

"So the problem is: how to catch Memlink by the tail?"

It was a difficult conundrum. He'd had police contacts set up a net for any clues, but he hadn't been able to grasp anything so far. *That nun, the sole survivor, may have seen the killer, but . . .*

"Sir Carrel?" A frail voice from the other side of the door stopped the Methuselah's train of thought. "It's Willem. We're back."

It was his baby brother's servant. A Terran. *So they've captured the witness safely.*

"Come in. Did you bring the nun?" he asked as he leaned back in his chair. But the Terran looked depressed when he entered the room, which did not bode well. Carrel sharply raised one eyebrow.

Behind the short Terran, other Terran servants brought in a red-stained stretcher. White sheets covered an irregular shape;

hanging to the side was a limp, bloodless hand. The hand, frozen as if grasping something, had a sapphire ring on it.

"I–is this some sort of joke?" Carrel stumbled toward the stretcher as it was placed under the bright chandelier. With a trembling hand, he took the sheet off, and gulped.

"Willem, explain! Is this a sick joke or what?!" Carrel yelled.

"Th–the priest . . ." the short Terran's voice cracked. "An amazingly strong priest intervened. He took down Sir Peter . . ."

"A *priest?!*" Carrel barked. He looked down at his baby brother's headless body. The cut was sharp and clean, right through one of few weak points a Methuselah had: the cervical vertebrae. Even the ageless, almost immortal vitality of the Methuselah would not survive such an attack. This was the job of an assassin who specialized in Methuselah killings. Carrel knew that the only organization that would employ such a monstrous killer was . . .

"So the Vatican is already here!" The outraged vampire, his eyes bloodshot with unshed tears, growled. "What the hell are you waiting for?! We must kill that priest! Get ready to go!"

"N–now, sir? The sun is about to come up soon. You shouldn't go out."

Carrel looked at the clock; the hands pointed to five o'clock. He clenched his teeth. Even though the sun came up late in the winter, there were only two hours before daybreak.

Should I wait until night? No! Then, should I let these Terran do it? But, if Peter was killed by this priest, then what can these Terran do?

"Ah, I have an idea." Carrel smiled.

One of the Terran servants said, "Wait. You mean that man we bought from Germanicus? Well, yes, we could use him . . . but, boss, are you sure?"

The short Terran looked up shyly. "If we let him out into the streets during daytime, he'd stick out for sure."

"I'll let the police know in advance. I've been paying them off in preparation for times like these."

Carrel bared his fangs and removed the ring from his brother's hand. "I don't care how many people die! I want you to bring back that priest and nun!"

II

Agnes woke up to a familiar sight. It was the ceiling of the bedroom in which she'd lived since she was five, back when the church had first took her in. "I'm . . . ow."

When she tried to get up, she flinched. A sharp pain went through her shoulder. As her hand instinctively touched where it ached, she felt a neatly wrapped bandage around it.

"Someone treated my wounds?"

Cautiously, she stood. The sun, now high in the sky, shone through the curtains. She had been asleep for a long time. Her recollection of what had happened after the vampire's claws dug into her shoulder was fuzzy. The only thing she could remember was blood spurting into the mist, and a dark figure standing far to the side.

She tilted her head as she pondered what had happened. Then, she heard something. It was a faint.

Agnes stepped out to the dark hallway.

She heard a grinding sound come from the chapel. She peeked between the slightly opened doors, but couldn't see anything other than the crucifix and the pipe organ against the wall.

No.

"H-he's . . . ?!"

Sunlight came through from the stained glass windows, showering a blond man in radiant colors.

He was young. He looked like he was in his mid-twenties. His tightly sculpted muscles were tense as he stood on his right hand, his left hand held out parallel to the ground, holding that staff of his. His right hand pumped up and down in a determined rhythm, his chin almost touching the ground, then he pushed high up into the air again. He did this repeatedly.

"Nine hundred ninety, nine hundred ninety-one . . . You're up already? How are you feeling?" the man asked.

"Eh?!" Agnes stepped back in surprise; her back hit the wall. She winced at the shock to her shoulder.

"Nine hundred ninety-two, nine hundred ninety-three . . . Watch out. You shouldn't be moving around just yet. Your wounds might open up." The young man continued his pushups as he warned the teary-eyed girl.

Agnes finally noticed the countless scars all over his body. They looked deep, like the scars were made by swords. But it was strange to see that both of his forearms had no markings, but were smooth as a baby's skin . . .

Then she realized she'd been staring at a man's body the entire time.

Agnes covered her eyes and asked, "Who are you?!"

"Nine hundred ninety-nine, one thousand. Done." The young man dipped his body lower than before, then pushed off to stand upright. It was a tireless and graceful move. After wiping the sweat off his upper body, he put on his black cloak.

Agnes startled in disbelief. "A *priest's* cloak?! S-so, that means you are . . . ?"

"My name is Hugue. I'm a wandering priest," the young man replied pleasantly as he carefully fixed his attire. "I was assigned by Rome to investigate the murders that happened last week. Sister Agnes, since you were the only survivor of this incident, I have a few questions to ask you . . . Oh, and I prepared breakfast over there. Would you care to discuss the matter while we eat?"

✝

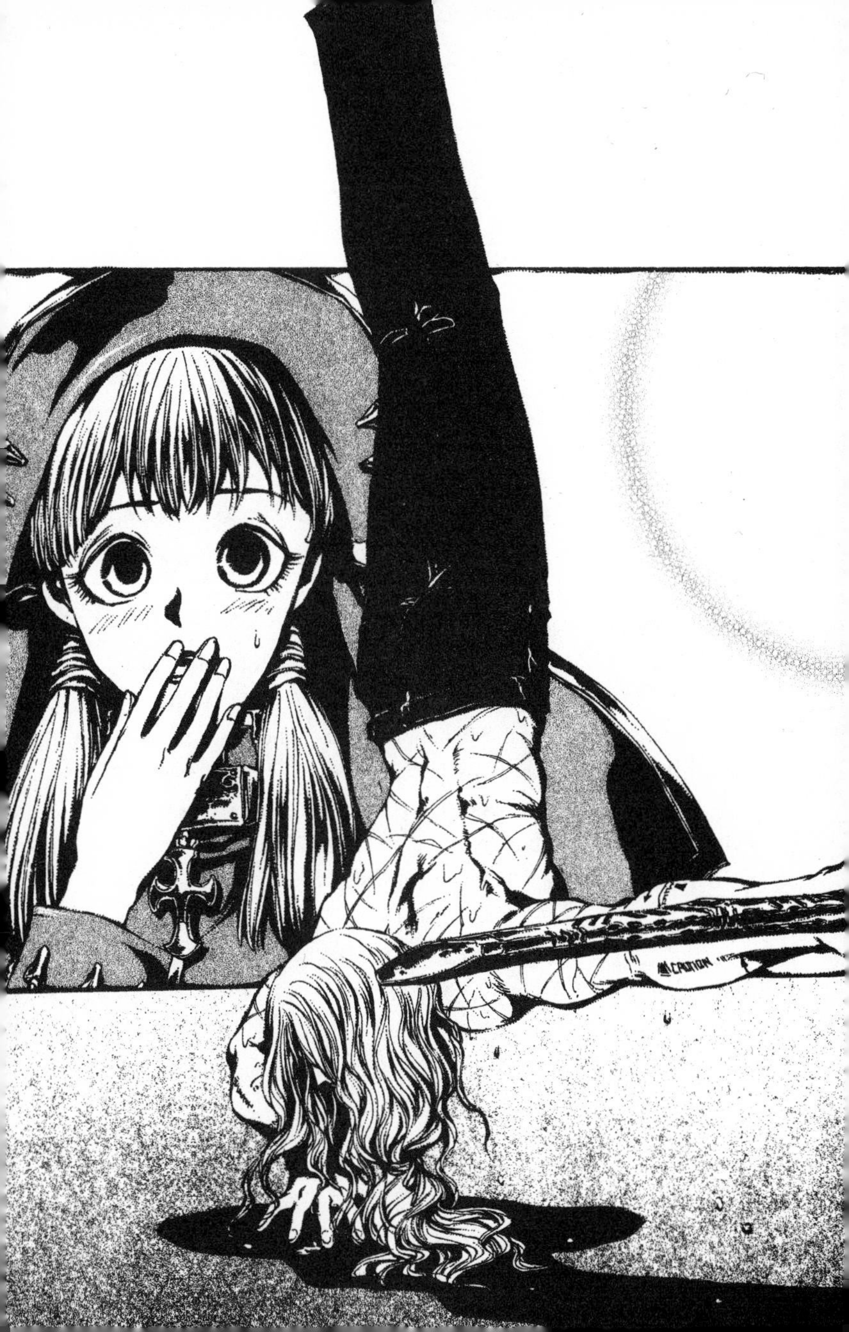
CAUTION

The meal wasn't luxurious, but nonetheless, it must have taken some time to prepare. In fact, it was a typical homemade breakfast often served in the Netherlands.

"I didn't mean to intrude, but I used your kitchen to cook this. I hope you can forgive me," he said.

"O-of course!" Agnes shook her head. *Come to think of it, how many days have passed since I ate a hearty meal?* After everyone was killed, she couldn't bring herself to make food. Besides, she really hadn't had much of an appetite since then . . .

"What's wrong, Sister Agnes? You're not going to eat?" he asked.

"Eh?" When she turned to see his worried look, she realized that tears had welled up in her eyes. Hastily, she rubbed them away. "No . . . no, I'm okay." Agnes shook her head again and sniffed. "I thought about everyone . . . I'm sorry, Father."

Hugue looked at the troubled girl's face, not knowing what to say; he placed his thick hand on her shoulder. "It was really unfortunate for all of those people to die," he said softly. "You started living in this church when you were a child, right?"

"Yes. My father used to be a knight. He came from a noble family . . . Are you familiar with the Watteau clan, Father?"

After drawing deep into his memory, he replied, "Somewhat."

The Watteau clan was a legendary noble family of the Netherlands; they'd employed many mercenaries. The clansmen kept the position of Chief Inspector for the Four-City Alliance over the generations, and subsequently held the largest military power over a government that had no actual national military. As a result, the Watteau family had great influence in political affairs. But that was all in the past. Nine years ago, in Bruges, a large-scale vampire attack annihilated the whole clan. The young nun's parents probably died with the rest of her clansmen.

"That night, I'd happened to catch a cold and was sent to my wet nurse's home. But when I heard about the tragedy, I was heartbroken. My parents and everyone I knew were killed back then; I was so sad . . . but I thought that it would be the last time I'd feel like that . . ." She couldn't hold back her grief any longer. Tears rolled down Agnes' cheeks. "It . . . happened again . . . !"

"I will avenge their deaths," he replied with conviction. "I will avenge the deaths of those who were close to you. Please leave that up to me . . . But before I fulfill this promise, please tell me, Sister Agnes . . . You returned to the scene right after it happened. Did you see anyone suspicious around Oude Kerk?" He handed her a napkin.

The girl, after dabbing her eyes and blowing her nose, shook her head. "I didn't see anyone . . . I told the police that several times already."

"Yes, I went over their reports. But if you hadn't seen anyone, then the pieces just don't add up . . . In other words, why would they attack you last night?" he asked.

"They?" Agnes looked up to see a picture that Hugue had placed before her. There was a man in the center of the fuzzy photo. He was large and had evil eyes and a hooked nose.

"Count of Amsterdam Carrel van der Verf—a vampire who controls the Amsterdam underground. Last night, he was the one who attacked. So, in essence, this vampire was after *you*," he said.

The nun froze, staring at the photo. "Wh-why? Why me?!"

"I don't know. At first, I thought they wanted to get rid of the witness. But if that were so, then they wouldn't have tried to kidnap you. This is my deduction, but . . . no, I won't go into it." He stopped.

"Umm, I don't think that last night was connected to . . ." *Should I say something that is probably unrelated to all this? But, it's the only thing I can think to talk about.* "That night, when I returned to the church, I went past a man."

"A man?"

"Yes. He looked like a noble with brown hair and mauve eyes, and he wore a gray coat . . . Oh, and he had some sort of flower tattoo on the back of his hand. But, if he was the murderer, then he should've killed me right there," she said.

The priest hugged his metal staff, lost in his thoughts. Soon enough, he looked up to Agnes. "Thank you. That helps . . . But you need to leave this town," he said.

"Eh?" the young girl uttered in surprise.

The priest warned her. "If you come with me to the station, you can make the express train. You must go to Rome tonight. The Vatican will keep you in protective custody until this case is solved. Oh, and when you get there, please help them draw the face of that man and send it to me," he ordered.

"N-no . . . Father, please let me kill those people, too! I promise not to get in your way! I want to kill them myself! I want to avenge all those deaths! Please!" she pleaded.

"No. You can't do that, Agnes." Hugue shook his head. "Until this case is solved, you must hide. It's for your own safety's sake."

"No! What's good for me is to—"

"Listen to me, Agnes," he interrupted coldly. His long fingers grabbed Agnes' sleeve. On the back of his hand, she saw a small tattoo—not quite a number or a letter.

The priest reasoned, "Once you stain your hands with someone's blood, no matter how much you despise them, there's no going back. 'A man who lives by the sword, dies by the sword.' Once you take someone's life, no matter how bad they were, the time will come when *you* will be hunted. You must keep using your sword, even in self-defense, and so you commit more sins. Eventually, though, one day you'll be killed by another's blade . . . That is the way of the sword. I don't want you to fall into that trap."

"Th-that's not fair!" Agnes yelled. She kicked her chair away. "Fine, I won't depend on you anymore, Father . . . I just can't forgive them!"

"Wait, where are you going?" he asked.

"It's none of your business!" Agnes snapped, turning her back on Hugue. "I'll avenge their deaths myself! Just leave me alone!"

"Don't do that. I can't allow it," Hugue said sternly. He reached out to grab her shoulder, but his fingers slipped. To be precise, his fingers jerked as if someone had pulled his arm away from her. "Damnation, not now!" Hugue muttered at his shaking hand. "Calm down, you. . ."

The young man, though he was so suave and collected in front of those vampires last night, was gritting his teeth now, trying to avoid sheer panic. But it had nothing to do with Agnes.

She took the opportunity to flee from the church.

"Wait, Agnes!" he called out.

She went out into the hallway. Seconds later, the wall exploded.

A fist punched through the wall and slammed her against the opposite side of the hallway.

"Hello, Sister." A shadow walked through the gaping hole and approached the breathless nun.

Agnes, squinting, struggled against the thick arm that held her. "An armored suit!"

A metal giant, over three meters high, had scooped up the immobile girl with one arm. It was a burly, swollen figure—an armored suit; a relic salvaged from pre-Armageddon technology. Simply put, it was an exoskeleton of armor.

"Agnes!" Hugue yelled.

"Good morning, Father . . . You really took good care of us last night." The suit's eyes glared back at the priest as he ran into the hallway. The voice ringing through the audio speakers sounded high-pitched and familiar. "Because of you, Carrel really chewed me out . . . Hey, drop that stinking weapon." The suit pointed at the staff with one hand, and tightened its hold on the girl with the other. "Hurry up and drop it. Otherwise, the girl will be crushed."

"D-don't, Father! Don—hrk!" Agnes choked. Her face reddened, and her lips started to turn blue from lack of oxygen.

"Okay," Hugue said in a low voice; his staff hit the floor, producing a loud, clear *twang*. "Don't touch the girl."

Agnes stared down at the staff as it rolled on the ground.

III

The underground chamber resembled an opera house.

Wide balconies protruded from the walls. About a dozen men and women wearing evening attire and expensive jewelry stood before a buffet table piled high with food. They laughed while busy waiters in black suits served chilled champagne. Below that, staircases led to the commoners' area, except tonight, the standing gallery was empty.

In the center of the chamber was a hollowed-out pit; it resmebled a coliseum, perhaps. The underground area was wider than a soccer field, and its floor was of smooth concrete. A metal fence surrounded the pit's perimeter. In the middle was a hole, probably for an elevator.

"Are you the surviving nun?" asked the robust man who occupied a large table by himself. As he stirred his fondue pot, he glared at Agnes. His thin eyes were full of anger and malevolence, and underneath his hooked nose was a matching set of curiously thin lips. He didn't seem very bright, but he did have a dangerous aura. "I'm Carrel van der Verf—I'm one of the Count Four who run Amsterdam. You know why you were brought here, right?"

"F-Father . . . where is Father Hugue?" Agnes, doing her best not to let her teeth chatter, glared back at the vampire with all her might.

"Don't worry. You'll see him in no time. So, anyway . . ." Carrel laughed out loud, and rolled Hugue's long staff onto the table. "Sister. Tell me about that incident. I heard from the priest himself. You saw the face of the killer, didn't you? What did he look like? Was it a man or a woman? A young or an old person? What did they look like?"

Agnes blinked rapidly. She thought she'd already told Hugue everything she knew. *Did the vampire not ask Father all this? Why did Hugue tell this man that I knew the killer's face, yet he didn't share the description . . . ?*

She finally realized—Hugue saved the details so she could be spared her life.

"Why aren't you saying anything? Speak. I'm short-tempered. If you talk, you'll be freed," urged Carrel, with a hint of uneasiness in his silver eyes.

"Before I tell you . . . where is Father Hugue? I won't talk until I see him," she demanded.

"Oh, so a Terran like you is trying to negotiate with me, Sister?" Carrel was irked. He lowered his voice. "You'd best speak up while I'm asking you nicely . . . Tell me, who killed those priests?!"

She almost fainted at the sight of his exposed fangs, but she stood her ground. "I must see Father! Otherwise, I won't tell!"

"What a stubborn brat." The vampire shook his head in disbelief. "If you want to see him that bad, here he is!"

Agnes heard a low, faint sound. She looked toward the coliseum and opened her eyes wide. "F-Father?!"

A large elevator rose in the center of the arena. The young man was standing in the middle. *But what did they do to him?*

Hugue was covered in blood from head to toe. It was a miracle that he was able to stand. On top of that, each of his ankles was chained, restricting his movement.

"Well, it's showtime!" Carrel snapped his thick fingers. With a rumbling sound, one of the walls of the arena opened up. Inside the opening was a dark cave—or rather, a corridor.

Agnes gulped and listened carefully. She heard a dull, metallic sound. It sounded like . . . footsteps.

A large, distorted humanoid figure appeared. The armored suit raised its left hand, which held a shield, and awkwardly saluted the noble section of the coliseum. It then pointed a mace, about the size of a small child, toward the priest.

"Begin." Carrel snapped his fingers again, and a black-clothed man blew a trumpet. Upon hearing the fanfare, the armored suit, though clunky, moved swiftly forward.

"Father!" As Agnes covered her face with her hands, the mace thundered down onto the ground. It smashed a crater into the floor. Chunks of fist-sized concrete flew about like grenade fragments.

But the priest wasn't there anymore. Somehow, he'd dodged the blow.

He dragged his chained feet along, running over to the armored suit's blind spot. But he moved slowly, like an elderly man. The armored suit, resembling a cat teasing its prey, forced the priest to the edge of the ring.

"Get away, Father!" Agnes yelled.

The mace swung up again. When Hugue tried to twist his body to dodge it, his shoulder bumped into the metal fence. The mace dropped onto his muscular back.

Hugue gasped in pain.

Reddish black liquid sprayed forth, and Hugue dropped to one knee. The armored suit didn't take another swing, but instead kicked the priest's stomach.

"S-stop . . . stop that thing!" she stuttered.

"Only if you cooperate, Sister." The vampire laughed. As he stirred the fondue pot, he licked his lips with his pointy tongue. "If you tell me who killed them, I'll free the priest."

A hoarse voice came from below. "Don't . . . Once you tell him, he'll kill you, too."

"Hmph, what an annoying bastard . . . Willem!" Carrel called out.

The armored suit raised one foot above the priest's head as if it would crush Hugue's skull like a fragile egg.

"What's wrong, Sister? If you don't talk fast, that priest's head will look like this cheese," Carrel said, indicating the contents of his melting pot.

Agnes looked back and forth to the metal staff and the bubbling pot. She pursed her lips. *This man is truly a devil. Both of us will be killed no matter what I say.*

She wanted to take back the mean things she'd said to the priest earlier. All she could do was to sit there and watch him suffer. The man she'd belittled had found the best way for her to survive, but she couldn't do anything to help him in return.

"Okay," she said.

"Don't, Agnes!" Though she could hear Hugue's cracking voice, Agnes pretended she hadn't.

"I'll tell you everything," she said.

"Good." Carrel leaned forward and rubbed his hands together like a fly. "So? What did the murderer look like?"

"When I returned to the church, a man walked past me. He had brown hair and mauve eyes . . . He had a cold look."

"Don't tell me it was Memlink?!" Without realizing that he'd interrupted her, Carrel turned and shouted to his men. "Did you hear that? So it was him, for sure!"

"Ca-Carrel!" a black-clothed Terran yelled out.

When Carrel turned back to see what his men were looking at, the hot contents of the fondue pot splashed onto his face. "Gah! Wh-why you little bitch!" Carrel cried out in pain.

A Terran might have been blinded, but it was nothing to an immortal Methuselah. It only caused him to temporarily lose sight for a second or two—but for Agnes, those few moments saved her life.

She jumped to grab the metal staff. Before Carrel could claw at it, she threw the surprisingly light weapon down into the coliseum.

As if it was God's will, the staff flew into Hugue's outstretched hand. He lay on his back, panting.

The girl called out to him as she looked down below. "Father . . . please fight!" Those were the only words she spoke. The next moment, sharp claws grated into her back and slammed her down onto the floor.

"You bitch!" Carrel scowled.

The nun fell down silently. The vampire stepped on her back and growled. He aimed a finishing blow at her exposed neck.

"Ca-Carrel, be careful!" the men said.

The armored suit that was prepared to crush the priest's head suddenly froze in place. Not only that, but . . .

"Wi-Willem?!" Carrel cried out.

It was an unbelievable sight. The upper body of the large armored suit bent at the hip and tumbled down to the floor. It was perfectly sliced at the trunk, red blood spurting out from the incision.

Beside the broken remnants of the armored suit, the priest stood up with his metal staff tucked under his arm like a crutch. The shackles binding his feet had also been sliced off.

"You're next, Carrel van der Verf." His cold, green eyes pierced right through the terrified vampire. Fear was an emotion rarely felt by Methuselah . . . but when the priest stared coldly at Carrel, he froze.

"Wait for me . . . I'm coming up," Hugue growled sternly.

"K-kill him! Shoot him!"

In response to Carrel's orders, the black-clothed men pulled out their guns. They pointed their muzzles toward the coliseum and squeezed their triggers. These professional gunmen were formerly cops and soldiers—they were excellent marksmen. The priest, standing in the center of the arena, should have been blown to pieces.

But a gray wall appeared in front of Hugue.

By the time they realized that it was his staff twirling rapidly, the rounds were ricocheting around the room. Simultaneously, the violently twirling metal fan was rapidly moving up toward the balcony.

"T-too fast . . . Hold your fire! You'll shoot each other—" The black-clothed man who called out to prevent friendly fire shrieked and spurted blood as the blade-staff suddenly struck through his throat.

A shadow, slipping past the falling corpse, jumped into the nobles' section of the coliseum. Before the men could fire again, Hugue's metal staff cracked their skulls, swatting each one down like an insect.

"Why, you pesky little Terran!" A noble lady in a blue dress threw her opera glasses to the side and stood up. Long claws stretched out from her slender, beautiful fingers.

"Die!" She scowled and thrust her right hand out, but Hugue blocked it with his staff. The lady's lips curled up, and her left hand tried to strike his face. Even a master like Hugue couldn't dodge that.

But Hugue didn't miss a beat. He moved his right hand slightly and the sound of metal sliding on metal reverberated throughout the underground chamber. There was a small crack in the metal staff. From that crack, there came an awesome white glow . . .

An air-splitting sound preceded a fountain of fresh, red blood. The lady's head rolled onto the table. Her body stood for a moment, then spurted blood and tumbled down the stairs.

The other Methuselah finally realized that they were in grave danger.

Hugue, cloaked in shadows, kneeled beside the unconscious nun. The black-robed priest was holding a saber with an extremely thin blade and graceful curve. It was radiant.

"What is that sword?!"

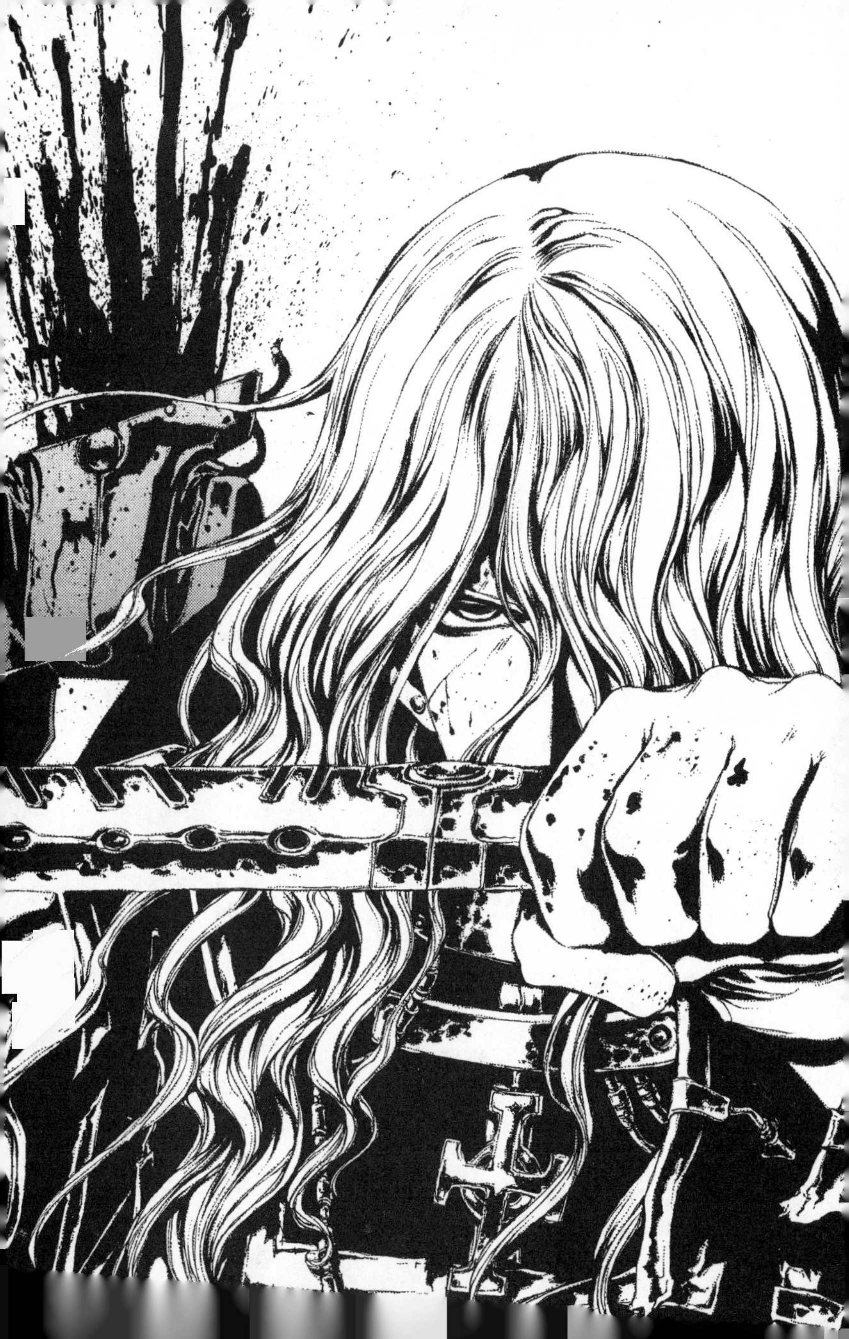

"I-I can't believe it. He killed a Methuselah with one stroke!"

While the other Methuselah panicked, Carrel maintained his dignity as a clan leader. He snarled, "How dare you kill my men? You're not a normal priest, are you?!"

Hugue was surrounded by more than ten vampires, but he didn't seem too concerned. The glowing blade in his right hand illuminated his face. He switched from a reverse grip to a forward grip and brought the sword up to his blue eyes. "My name is Hugue de Watteau. I am an AX agent . . ." He whirled his blade around. "Code name Sword Dancer!"

"AX Agent . . . ? So, you're a Vatican assassin!" Carrel yelled.

The priest came up behind one of the Methuselah and pierced his blade through the young vampire's heart. As his sword swung up through the man's neck, it sliced diagonally through the Methuselah's collarbone, creating another curtain of blood.

"Haste mode! Use haste mode to get him!" Carrel ordered.

The Methuselah never imagined that a lowly Terran could kill one of their own.

Carrel barked at the younger ones. "He's only a Terran! Use your haste mode!"

The ultimate power of a Methuselah was to hyperactivate its nervous system to increase speed. Because it burned up the body's energy, they couldn't use it for long periods of time, but Carrel figured they probably only needed three seconds to crush this menace. The older Methuselah went into haste mode, slipped past the dead young Methuselah, and tried to attack the priest's vulnerable back. His fangs extended to dig into Hugue's neck like a wolf about to kill its prey—

"What?!" His fangs met thin air. The priest was gone. "Where did he . . . ?"

"You waste too much time in your movements," Hugue whispered into the vampire's contorted face as his long blade-staff stabbed through Carrel's heart. "And you underestimate humans."

"Te-Terran . . . !" Although the blade twisted around and burst his heart, the old vampire still resisted death with all his might. He grabbed the sword that poked out of his chest with both hands.

He should have died by now, but his will to fight caused his heart to contract and lock the sword in place. "Die, Terran!"

Carrel closed in on the weaponless priest. The vampire strained, reached out, and grabbed a battleaxe from the wall.

Hugue reached for his empty sheath just as the heavy axe aimed straight for his head!

There was a momentary clash of metal.

In Hugue's hand was a blade, blocking the axe. Carrel realized that it was a small dagger pulled out from the other end of Sword Dancer's sheath, but by the time he'd figured that out, his upper body had contorted grotesquely. He was pushed back by the priest's fierce strength.

"Urgh!"

Despite the unnatural position, the Methuselah was able to take another swing at Hugue, trying to bring the axe down upon the priest's head one last time. But by then, Hugue had pulled his long blade from the vampire's body.

"Too slow!" Hugue said, pulling the sword under his right arm.

Images of the deaths he'd caused and the deaths he would cause in the future flashed through Hugue's mind. He even thought of his own impending death—but he wasn't going to die *now*.

With a piercing shout, Hugue kicked the ground and sprang forward. He flung his sword up with one hand to parry the axe. *"Omnes enim qui acceperint gladium, gladio peribunt.* Those who live by the sword, die by the sword. Amen!"

The sword maintained its speed and thrust into the screeching vampire's throat.

✝

The flesh wounds on the girl's back were deep enough to see some of her bones. She'd be okay for now, but she needed treatment as soon as possible. She'd survive, but she might be scarred for life.

"I'll take you to the hospital . . . You'll be fine. I won't let you die." Hugue picked the young girl up and carried her away from the carnage.

"Did he die?" Agnes, though in a lot of pain, was able to open her eyes a bit. "Did you . . . kill him, Father Hugue?"

"No, not yet," he answered.

The long blade had pinned Carrel to the wall. It had missed the cervical vertebrae by several microns. A Methuselah wouldn't die easily until its vital point was destroyed. If Carrel moved an inch, the blade would end his life.

"What shall we do? If you'd like, we can kill him. Do you want to seek revenge?" Hugue asked.

Agnes moved her injured neck as best she could. She looked down at Hugue's bloodied hands. She replied sadly, "No."

Her cheek twitched when she tried to smile. "No, I won't seek revenge."

"Good choice," Hugue replied sincerely. "I'll take you to the hospital immediately. Go to sleep for now."

Hugue laid Agnes on the ground, stood, and fixed his attire. He had to do one more thing before he took the girl to the hospital.

"Answer me, Carrel van der Verf." The priest's voice was suddenly cold, completely different from the way he'd spoken to the girl. "Why did you ask Sister Agnes about the murders? Didn't one of your own men do it?"

"Hell if I know." The weak vampire opened his eyes. He couldn't move a thing below his neck. "Framed . . . I was framed . . . by Memlink . . ."

"Framed? Do you mean Antwerp's Hans Memlink? Is he the murderer?" Hugue asked.

"Maybe . . . Help me . . . I didn't attack Oude Kerk, I swear," Carrel gasped.

Even though he might not be guilty of attacking the church, a Vatican priest couldn't just let a scheming vampire go free.

Carrel continued to plead with tears in his eyes. "I . . . I really don't know a thing . . ."

"Then answer one more question about the Watteau clan murder. If you are honest, I'll help you. If not . . ." His fingers touched the long blade-staff. "Tell me. Did you attack the Watteau clan? Which vampire killed the parents, sliced off the son's arms, and kidnapped the daughter?!" Hugue demanded. "Who killed everyone and took my sister Anies?!"

Carrel's eyes rolled to the back of his head. "A Terran named Jan van Maylen asked us to attack Bruges. He hired us . . ."

"Jan van Maylen? The master of the Maylen clan?! Don't lie! They're *kin* of the Watteau clan!" Hugue protested.

"No lie. He was after the post of Chief Inspector that the Watteau clan held for a long time . . . Heh, the Terran consider us to be monstrous, but look at them," Carrel said.

"Who actually attacked the house?" Hugue asked, gripping the hilt of sword so tightly that his hand shook. "Answer me, Carrel. This is my final question. What is the name of the vampire who attacked the Watteau clan?"

"The guy who did it was . . . was . . ."

Hugue instinctively dodged something hurtling from behind. It was a thick arrow.

"No!" Though he successfully dodged it, Hugue cried out in disbelief. The large gray arrow had struck Carrel and instantly killed him.

When Hugue turned around, a gray-coated shadow looked down at him. Half of the figure's face was covered by a large-brimmed hat and a silver mask. But when their gazes met, the masked man's mauve eyes seemed to be laughing at Hugue.

"Wait!" Hugue shouted.

But the gray-coated figure disappeared into the dark hallway. Hugue wanted to follow him, but he looked back at the unconscious girl, who lay bleeding on the ground.

If he left her now, she would surely die.

Every heartbeat brought her closer to death. He took off his priest's robe and pulled her up.

"Just hang on." He had no time to waste. The priest began to run out of the coliseum, hazarding one last glance back at the dark hallway.

"I will never give up."

✝

"This is regarding the case of serial murders on passenger ships in Albion waters," said Sister Kate as she read the analysis report. "This is a very touchy subject. There's a possibility that one of the Albion nobles is part of a scandal. This might be the most information that normal staff could uncover."

"So we might need special staff for this case . . . That means we lose another body." Caterina stood near the window and sighed.

Once the sun rose, the air became warm. Spring sunshine filled Saint Peter's Plaza, and the worshippers wore light clothing.

"I guess we have no other choice. Albion is one of the top two secular countries. And we still owe them on the kidnapping case . . . We should be extra careful and dispatch two special agents. Crusnik and Sword Dancer are available, right?" Caterina asked.

"W-well . . ." Sister Kate muttered.

"What's the matter?" Caterina looked concerned at her subordinate's unusual hesitation. *Am I mistaken?*

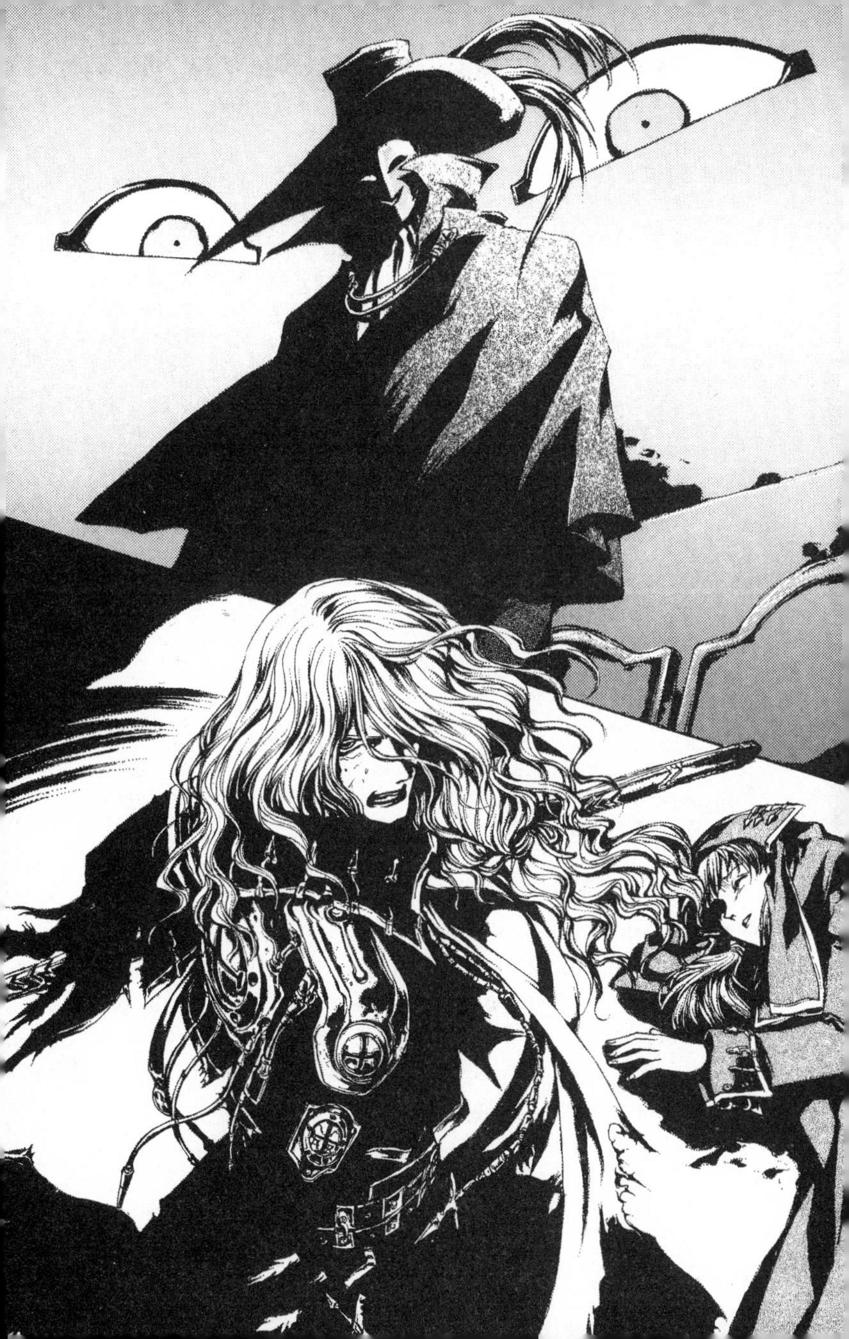

"Cardinal, Sword Dancer has not returned to Rome yet."

"What do you mean? The report on the vampire killings was received two weeks ago. I just assumed he had taken some time off, but where is he now?" she demanded.

"Y-yes. You are correct, but . . ." The nun drooped her gaze. "Father Hugue reported that there were no suspects among the killed vampires. He mentioned that it was necessary to continue the investigation in Antwerp."

Caterina sighed. "I read the report. That's why the investigators are following up on that case. We were supposed to dispatch an AX agent once we found something significant. Is there something wrong with that?"

"He wasn't satisfied with that plan and went to Antwerp himself . . . I-I'm so sorry!" Sister Kate apologized.

The cardinal pounded her desk. "How dare he run off like that?!" After venting her disappointment, she calmed down a bit, but her eyes were still cold.

Sister Kate asked sheepishly, "Umm, so what shall we do, Cardinal?"

"Tell Crusnik to get Dandelion out of the cage. Let's have those two take care of the Albion case," Caterina said.

"Er, I was asking about what to do with Sword Dancer," said Sister Kate.

The cardinal played with the rosary that hung about her neck as she thought for a moment. It was her call to send Hugue to the Netherlands, despite the risks involved. Also, she was aware of the ongoing Amsterdam case. "Keep sending out return orders to Sword Dancer. If he complies, then I will not punish him for violating regulations. *This* time."

"Roger. I will pass that on to him," Sister Kate replied.

"Thank you. Oh, and Sister Kate?" Caterina added.

The nun was relieved, but she froze upon hearing the next question.

"So, what is the progress of the Milan case? Please ask the Professor how long it will take Gunslinger to fully recover."

EXTRAS

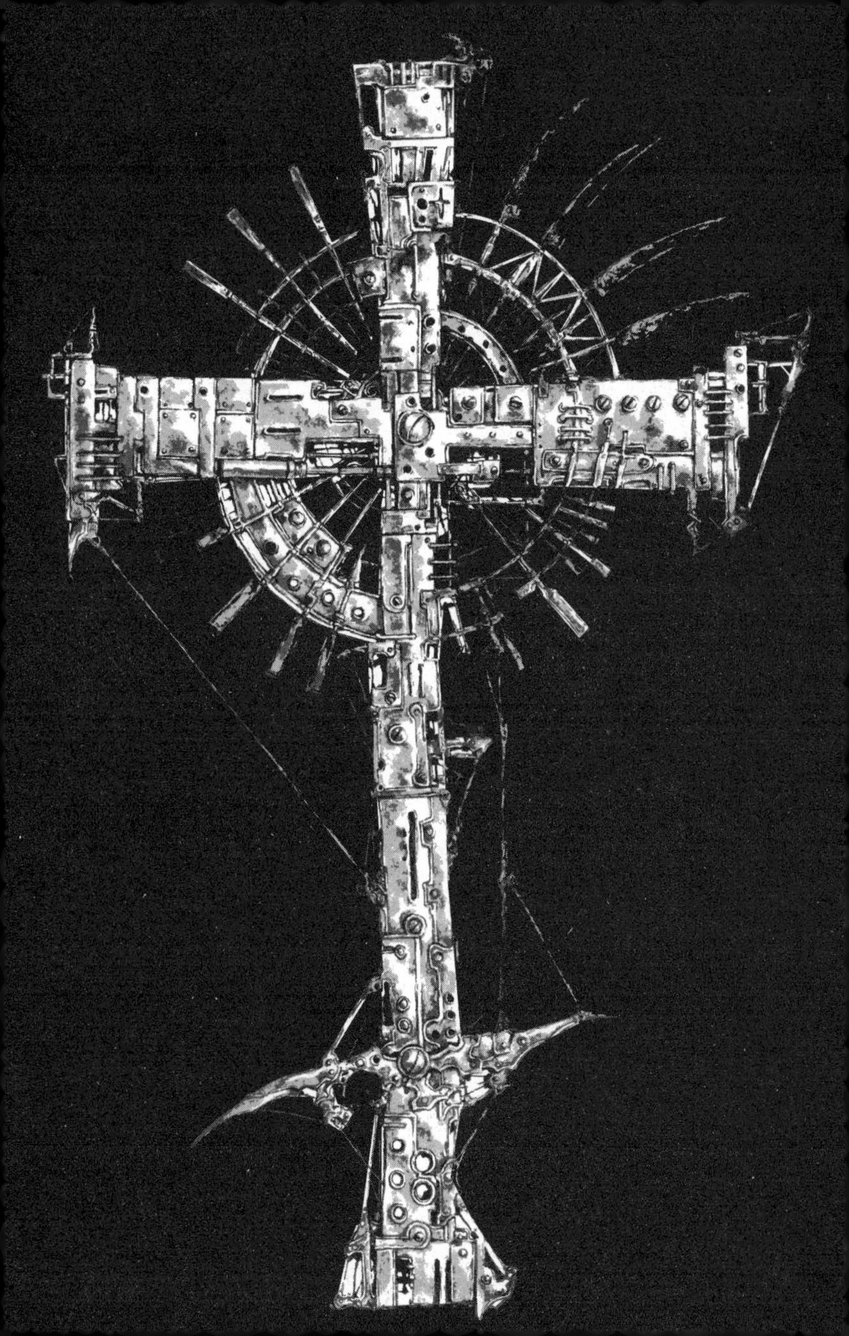

The World of Trinity Blood

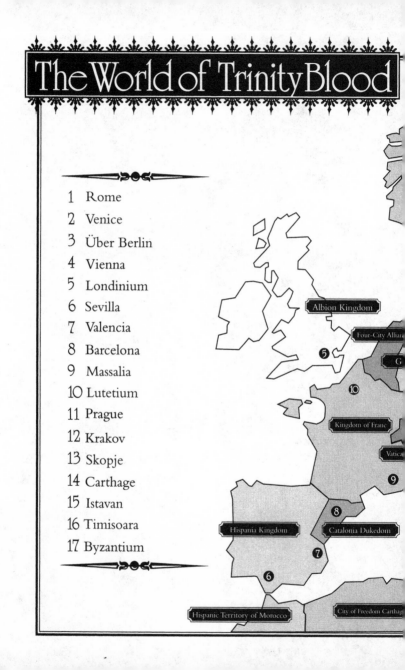

Albion Kingdom

Four-City Allian

G

Kingdom of Franc

Vatica

Hispania Kingdom

Catalonia Dukedom

Hispanic Territory of Morocco

City of Freedom Carthag

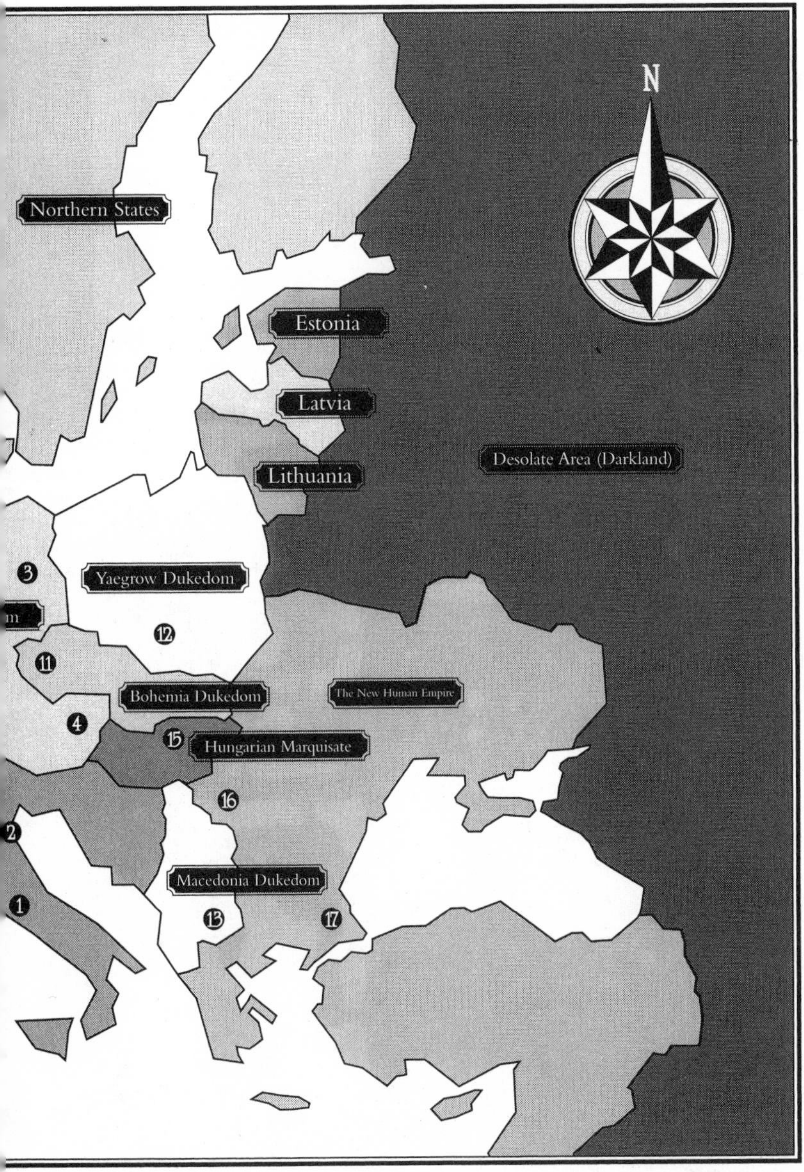

N
Northern States
Estonia
Latvia
Lithuania
Desolate Area (Darkland)
Yaegrow Dukedom
m
3
12
11
Bohemia Dukedom
The New Human Empire
4
15
Hungarian Marquisate
16
2
Macedonia Dukedom
1
13
17

The heart, with
permanent scars
The body, with haunted marks
To atone for the mortal sins
Must you walk the dark
path again today?

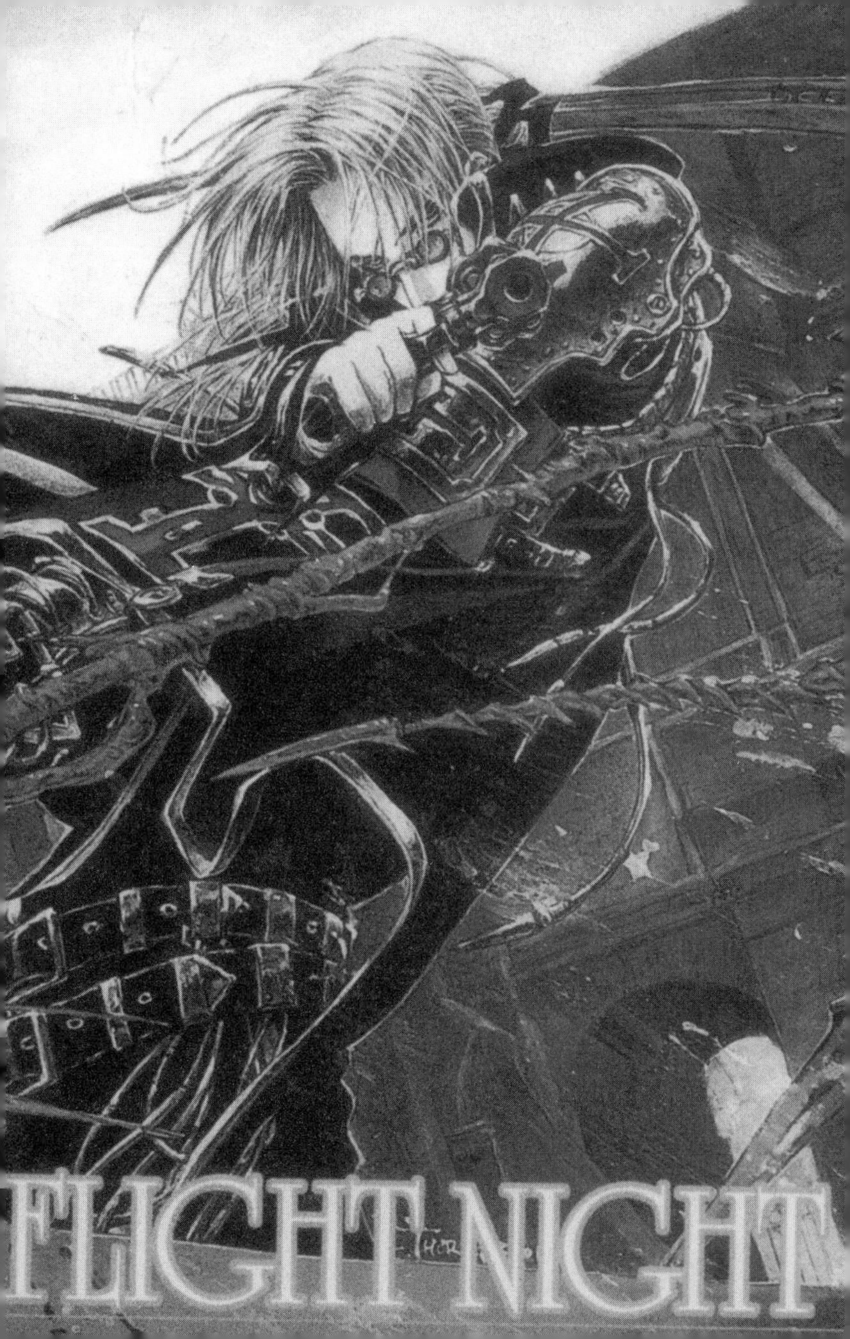
FLIGHT NIGHT

The wrath of God shall fall
upon those who go against
His Will

He who is wrapped in
powdery smoke

Death throes resonate

The steel hound
released from
its chains

Curtains
rise for the
massacre opera

WITCH HUNT

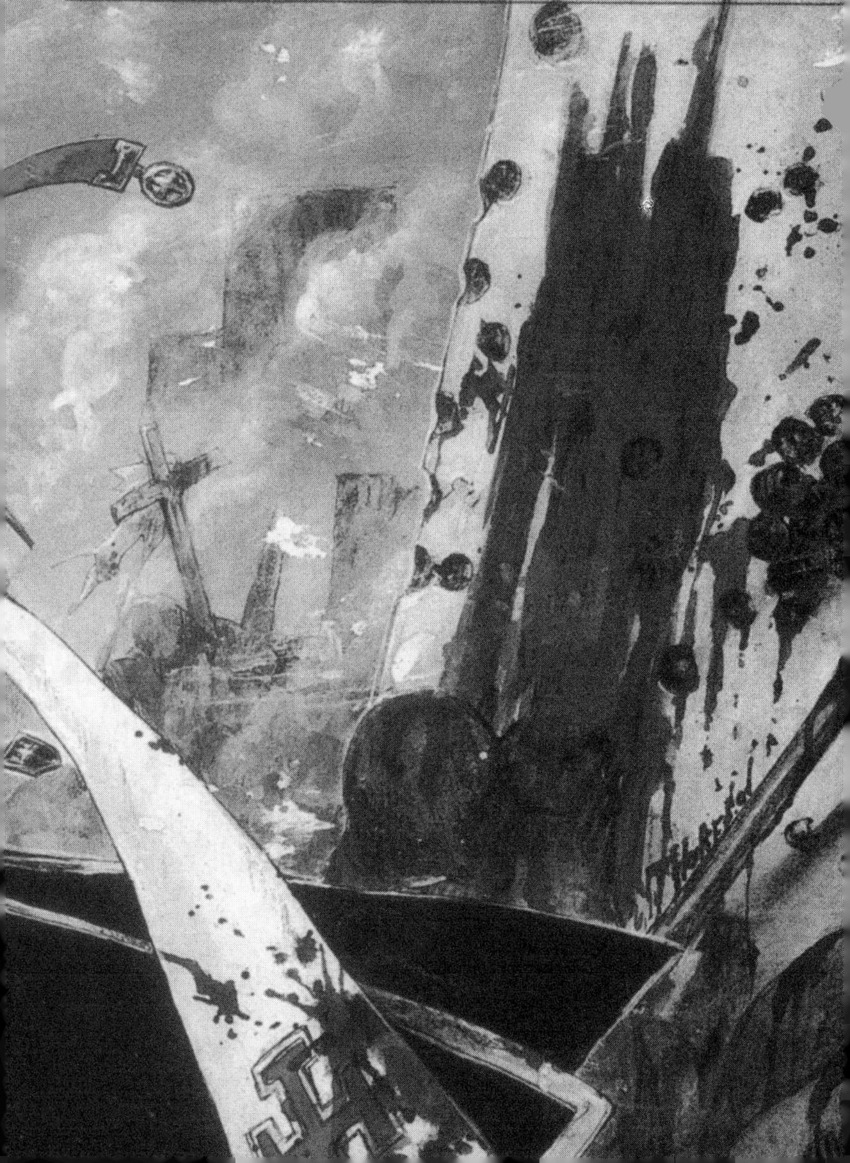

FROM THE EMPIR

Coming from an
inhuman country
Beautiful princess
of a foreign origin
Images of the
human world
in her amber eyes
What does it tell her?

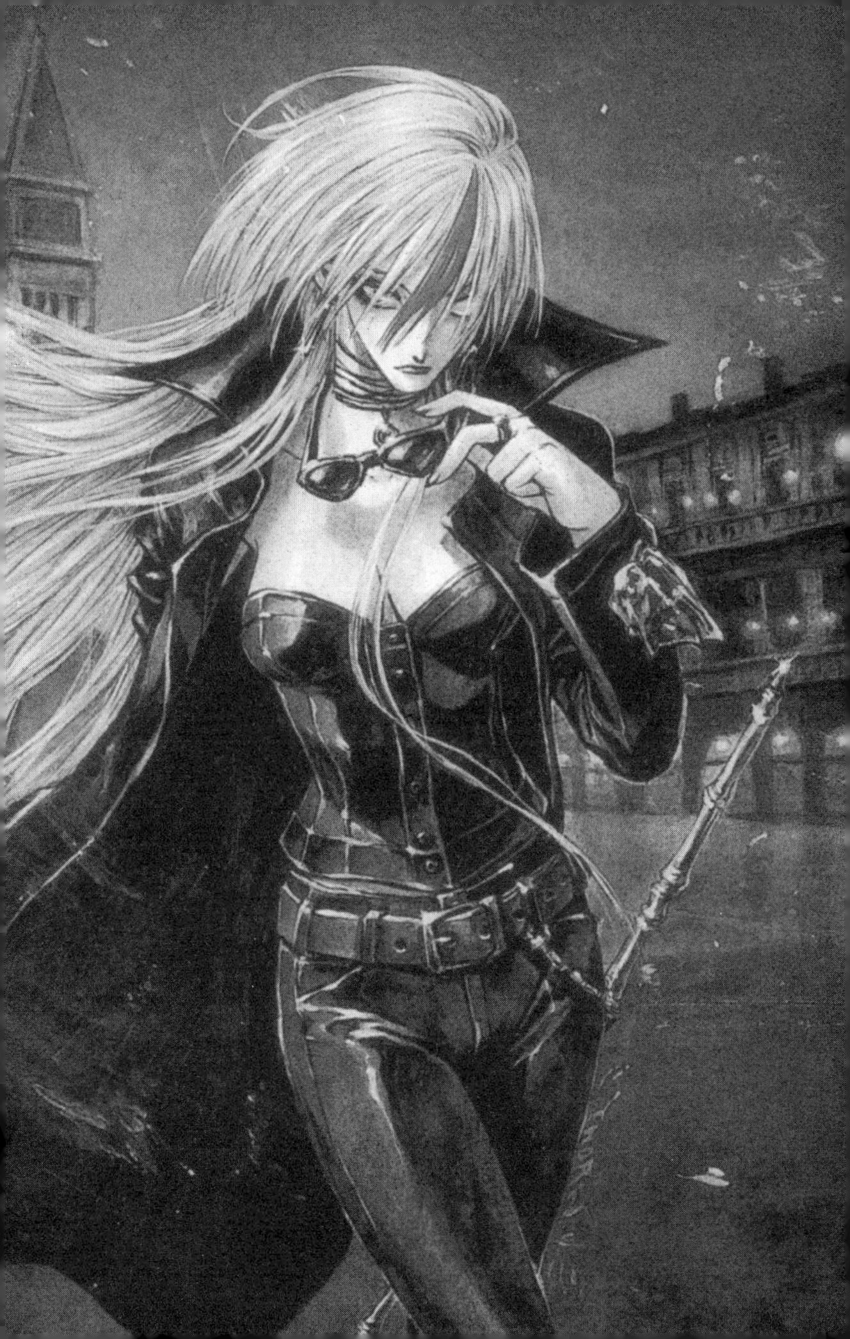

You, who controls
the night
Hidden inside the
lovely girl's body
Is it a diabolic,
horrendous monster
Or the maternal lov[e]
that surrounds
everything?